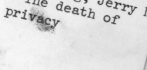
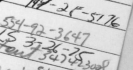
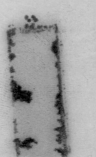

by Jerry M. Rosenberg

Automation, Manpower and Education

The Computer Prophets

New Conceptions of Vocational and Technical Education

The Death of Privacy

JERRY M. ROSENBERG   5 ᵐ 2553

The
Death of
Privacy

RANDOM HOUSE : NEW YORK

FIRST PRINTING

9 8 7 6 5 4 3 2 1

Library of Congress Catalog Card Number: 69–16448
Manufactured in the United States of America
by The Book Press, Brattleboro, Vermont.
Designed by Cynthia Krupat

Special thanks and acknowledgment to the following for permission to
reprint:

The RAND Corporation—From H. Petersen and R. Turn's "Systems Implications of Information Privacy," April 1967, and Paul Baran's "Communications, Computers and People," November 1965.

System Development Corporation—From the July–August 1967 issue of *System Development Corporation Magazine.*

Business Week—From "Computers, How They're Remaking Companies," February 29, 1964, and "Computers Put Speed into the Law," October 1, 1966.

Management Science Publishing, Inc.—From various issues of *Automatic Data Processing Service Newsletter.*

The Atlantic Monthly and Bob Elliott and Ray Goulding—From "The Day the Computers Got Waldon Ashenfelter," November 1967, Copyright © 1967 by the Atlantic Monthly Company, Boston, Mass. Reprinted with permission.

To Lauren and Elizabeth

PREFACE

When Adolf Hitler was aspiring to the Chancellorship of Germany, he acquired the confidential European Census and used it to weed out some of his potential antagonists.

With the advance of technology, centralized data accumulation becomes easier, the reward for intrusion is increased, and control shifts to still fewer people.

Should we not be concerned about a computerized federal data center that could collect, store and distribute information about every one of us? Although the data may be acquired in a Constitutionally sound fashion, its use could present the greatest threat to our remaining right to individual privacy.

Likewise, as computerized data facilities are established in nongovernmental institutions, the issue of privacy and information leakage may become more explosive since laws are less able to enter the hidden corridors and file systems in industry, labor and education. In the private sector, management's disinterest in the privacy issue or in safeguards of data retrieval may invite resistance.

The informed public and the student protestor have been demanding the opportunity to speak their minds without fear of long-range consequences affecting employment and future paths of behavior. Removing the right to privacy can lead to a conforming society fearful of experimenting with the challenges of the day.

This book proposes to examine the capability of computers and computerized data banks to evolve the most efficient and accurate documenting, never-forgetting system known to man. No attempt shall be made to deny the value of data collection or deny the worth of computerization. The point of concern is that without sufficient effort to inject adequate safeguards, to have the opportunity to refute stored personal information, to allow the individual to determine what is collected, to maintain a permanent check on how data are used, we may some day stop asking whether our privacy is being invaded— when that time arrives we will find that we have no privacy left to invade.

Jerry M. Rosenberg
September 1, 1968
New York City

ACKNOWLEDGMENTS

Grateful acknowledgment is given to those who have been encouraging and helpful in the development of this book. Too many to name, members of the Senate and House of Representatives, computer specialists, psychologists, lawyers, industrialists and professors offered suggestions that were invaluable in the formation of numerous concepts and recommendations.

In particular, I would like to thank Professor Alan Westin and my former graduate students from Columbia University for reading the original manuscript. To my editors, John Simon and Alice Mayhew, and my copy editor, Cordelia Jason, a word of deepest appreciation for their support in this project and expertness in discharging their responsibilities. To my wife, Ellen, for her patience and understanding which were essential catalysts throughout the past years during the writing of this book.

CONTENTS

The Death of Privacy

CHAPTER I

The All-Seeing Eye

"The central problem of the age is the scientific revolution and all the wonders and the damage it brings," spoke Supreme Court Justice William O. Douglas. What are the rights of men against the increasingly important machine? Are new Constitutional amendments needed to maintain our liberty?

Justice Douglas suggests that our original legal protections are failing to provide the appropriate guarantees of human rights in a period of accelerating science and technology. The needs of government and bureaucracy are so great that our assumed rights to freedom and privacy may be slipping away without any noticeable public protest. "If the Bill of Rights were being written today," said that Justice, "it also would encompass some of the recurring evils arising out of the vast exercises of authority through the administrative agency."[1] (In fact, the original Bill of Rights contains no mention of the word *privacy*.)

Some people have long recognized that fewer and fewer people are gaining more and more power in determining the ultimate course of the American way of life. Former President Eisenhower in a speech at Defiance College in Ohio stated boldly that Americans had succumbed to ". . . an unthinking abandonment of personal and local responsibility to a few men in government, giving to them a frightening power for ◄

Both of these statements were made in the early 1960s when ◄ good or evil—and almost certain to invite error or abuse."[2] the issues of privacy and freedom were rarely associated with the enormous potential of computer machines, and few gave much thought to the idea of a massive computerized federal data bank.

All national agencies use computers, and manufacture a giant system to absorb the growing amount of collected information. They retain a form of independence by operating their own systems, and seldom allow confidential data to be circulated among other interested federal departments.

The U.S. Civil Service Commission maintains a file on almost everyone who has ever applied for federal employment since 1939. Its central index system houses approximately 7,500,000 files. The Internal Revenue Service handles over 400 million documents a year. In 1930 only 6 million tax returns had to be checked; by 1970 it is projected that there will be as many as 114 million. All data processing for the IRS is now conducted in its National Computer Center which holds a master file of 80 million taxpayer accounts stored on magnetic tapes. Since the system requires the identification of taxpayers, Social Security numbers are used on all statements.

In 1964 IRS reported a $2 billion increase in interest income, i.e., bank deposit interest; this was a rise of 28 per cent over 1963. They credited this to the public's awareness of what the use of computers might mean in terms of possible detection. Collection from tax-delinquent businesses also increased after computers had been installed.

◄ At present, a national computer system is planned that will have an almost limitless capability to store, intermingle and, at the push of a button, retrieve information on persons, organizations and a variety of their activities, all without the knowledge of those involved. Even now, stacks of punched cards and tapes store statistics about us that we may not know exist.

Under the surveillance of a national data bank or center,

most of our actions could be documented, put into a permanent dossier and stored on tape along with other vital data about us. Here it would always be available at the push of a button. We would never escape in time or distance the bureaucratic machinery keeping tabs on us.

Can a computerized data bank harm us? The answer should be *no*, unless the retrieved information shows that we have broken the law; but in practice this yardstick might not apply. At present when we are accused of wrong-doing we have an attorney to look out for our interests. He protects us by demanding to know the reasons for arrest and, by calling witnesses, challenges the accusation. The plans for a federal data bank do not include informing an individual of the information filed under his name; thus there would be no opportunity for an attorney, for cross-examinations—there would be no recourse.

Will the plans be changed so an individual will know exactly what has been tabulated and kept on file? Will he be able to refute or challenge facts he believes to be in error, out of context, or confused by circumstance? Will he have a chance to reply to a potential employer who has just denied him a position because his complete dossier contains confidential aspects of his life that the employer finds "impossible to overlook"? Will we lose our present right to limit the circulation of personal information about ourselves? Will the right of privacy remain as the last dimension of man's true freedom?

If there are no safeguards in the method of collecting and the use of data filed away in computerized data banks, we may lose what have always been interpreted as Constitutional rights, that we take for granted. The right "to be let alone" may be slipping away without public protest. Voicing the fear that machines could dominate man, Dr. Simon Ramo, at the 150th anniversary of the New York Academy of Sciences in the fall of 1967, said, "It is this prospect that threatens the world with a robot society."[3]

:

The main inquiry into a proposed federal data bank began in 1966. On July 23, 1966, a special issue of *The Saturday Review* was devoted to a look at automation and the New

Computerized Age. One of its articles, "Automated Government
—How Computers Are Being Used in Washington to Streamline Personnel Administration to the Individual's Benefit,"[4] by
John W. Macy, Jr., Chairman of the U.S. Civil Service Commission, created a furor and became the focus of attention of
a Congressional hearing. For the first time the public was
brought into this growing controversy.

A special subcommittee of the U.S. House of Representa-
tives' Committee on Government Operations began an investigation into proposals to establish a national data center on
July 26, 1965, in the Rayburn Office Building, Washington,
D.C. Hon. Cornelius E. Gallagher, Congressman from New
Jersey and chairman of the subcommittee, presided, and Representatives Benjamin S. Rosenthal and Frank Horton, both of
New York, were present. This was the second phase of a two-
part inquiry into the general question of invasion of privacy.
The computerized age was described by Gallagher in his
opening warning, "The problem is potentially serious; its advance solution urgent."[5] These facts emerged from the subcommittee's investigation:

1. There are some twenty departments or agencies in the
federal system currently collecting and publishing data,
including the Internal Revenue Service, the Bureau of the
Census, the Office of Education, the Bureau of Labor
Statistics and the Bureau of Old-Age and Survivors Insurance. Information has been supplied to these groups by
individuals with the understanding that it will only be
used by the receiving agency for a specific purpose, and
in most cases on a confidential basis.

2. It is now planned that much of this information be
pooled into one central reservoir—a national data bank.*
Although current disclosure restrictions should be adhered
to, the effectiveness of these protective laws is somewhat
dubious. In the final analysis, the soundness and safety
of the system would remain in the hands of those who
control it.

* It has also been referred to as a national data center, federal statistical
data center and federal statistical service center.

3. With present technical capability, it is possible to develop a composite picture of an individual that can be stored in a single information warehouse. Each year we offer information about ourselves which becomes part of the record. It is often scattered across the continent and is usually inaccessible except after considerable effort. It begins with our birth certificate and is followed by a series of medical notations. Early in life we are documented as an added income tax deduction by our parents. Then there is information on what high school, public or private, and what college, public or private, we attended. At school, records are made of our abilities, grades, intelligence and attendance. For some, there will be car registration and driver's license, draft status, military service or Peace Corps. Then job history is recorded: working papers, Social Security number, a first job, our performance with each employer, recommendations, and references—all this makes an interesting dossier. Then, perhaps, a marriage license, a home mortgage, and when children come, the cycle begins anew. Should we divorce, the court records will be added. These would increase should we be arrested, convicted or serve time in prison. And of course when we die, a last footnote is made.

→ In our daily activities we leave behind a trail of records: the credit card carbon for a luncheon meeting, the receipt from the hotel where we spent last night, our airline ticket, the check we cashed in a city bank, and the bill for the toys we charged for our children.

There are also tax returns over a number of years, responses to increasingly lengthy census questionnaires, Social Security records, passport applications and perhaps our fingerprints. If we have worked for a defense contractor or for the federal government, there are lengthy files on us that may note our associations and affiliations. If we have applied for an FHA loan on a home, there will usually be an estimate of the prospects that our marriage will hold together.

Information is power. These records may at various times be of considerable interest to people outside a specific federal agency. Years after our birth, for example, an interested party

may be happy to pay for information from our birth certificate, which officially is confidential. And in a number of cities
there are entrepreneurs who obtain and sell this information,
as well as hospital records, police records, immigration records,
passport records and so on.

What is the threat of a central data bank? Past events have
shown us how powerful such pools of information can be.
Non-benevolent power seekers in history have taught us some
severe lessons about the use of available masses of data. An
example of this was Hitler's use of the European Census to
extract data on any citizen of the German Republic.

It should be remembered that when the Social Security
number was originated thirty-three years ago, it was a confidential reference. Now it is freely given when requested by
just about anybody. In fact, almost every major form requests
it. Recently, the American Bankers Association recommended
to its 13,600 member banks the use of Social Security numbers
as the basis of a country-wide personal-identification system.
Serial numbers of 400,000 sailors and marines in the armed
forces have been replaced with Social Security numbers in
military computer files.

Federal tax returns are supposed to be confidential, but
there are people other than the Internal Revenue agent who
can look at them. The federal government exchanges tax data
with forty-three states and the District of Columbia as well
as several committees of Congress. These data are released
only for a specific purpose in the "line of duty," and the
recipient is requested to follow rigid procedures designed to
keep the contents confidential. But there are cases that show
this confidence is being violated.

Senator Edward Long has noted that all our names together
have appeared in the files 2,800 million times. Information is
held in fourteen different federal agencies that have files on
each American. "Our Social Security numbers are listed 1,500
million times; other figures include: police records—264,500,-
000, medical history—342 million, and psychiatric history—
279 million.

"But what is of concern to us, however, are the following
discoveries: many agencies require individuals to divulge

personal information and yet give no pledge and are under no requirements to keep this information confidential. Included in this category are: court actions or involvements—19,253,000; security reports—17,693,000; psychiatric history—107,000."[6] Long found that many government agencies were collecting more personal and intrusive data than even the most open-minded informed individual could support. In addition, it was found that a considerable number of the files were not legally safeguarded against leakage.

Senator Strom Thurmond has also commented on this mania for collecting data: ". . . I think the public and the taxpayers might as well recognize the fact that when the Government continues to go more and more into every facet of people's lives, literally every phase of activity, which was never envisioned by those who wrote the Constitution, that there are going to be more and more requests for information because the more you approach the welfare state, the more information the bureaucrats have to have to make their reports. So it is conceivable that there will have to be more redtape and more records than there used to be when the Constitution was followed."[7]

Our laws have served us in many ways and in particular are most protective of us against attack by others. Must not technology be subject to these laws? Admiral Hyman Rickover says: "Technology must therefore conform to that most basic of all human laws, the maxim of the 'mutuality of liberty,' the principle that one man's liberty of action ends where it would injure another. . . . How in the future to make wiser use of technology is perhaps the paramount public issue facing the electorates of industrial countries. . . . There is need for laws requiring that before a particular technology may be used, reliable tests must have been made to prove it will be useful and safe."[8]

Confronted with the erosion of his privacy, the individual American has until now had the consolation that all these files have been widely dispersed and often difficult to put together. It has been a time-consuming, expensive proposition to compile a sizable file on any individual. Giant computers with their capacity for instant recall of a great variety of available information are changing all this. Representative Gallagher pleaded, "The presence of these records in Government files is frightening enough, but the thought of them neatly bundled together into one compact package is appalling. We cannot be certain that such dossiers would always be used by benevolent people for benevolent purposes."[9]

There have been several protections from those who might choose to invade our privacy. For one thing, it was difficult to obtain and gather information that had not been carefully organized. Before computers, techniques of assembling data in a meaningful fashion were insufficient. In any case, the time and effort involved were formidable. Until now, it has also been difficult to document accurately new information about an individual. Before the computer, it was nearly impossible to follow an individual without hiring a detective full-time. With ease of movement and a population of 200 million, people were able to lose themselves in the crowd. Surveillance was a difficult and expensive matter.

A combination of protective laws and the dispersion of records throughout the country has meant that no one person has possessed the power to draw together all the data concerning a citizen.

Oscar Ruebhausen and Orville Brim, Jr., in "Privacy and Behavioral Research," an article in the *Columbia Law Review*, wrote: "Computerized central storage of information would remove what surely has been one of the strongest allies of the claim to privacy—the inefficiency of man and the fallibility of memory."[10]

The possible future storage and regrouping of such personal information strikes at the core of our Judeo-Christian concept of "forgive and forget," because as any computer specialist knows, the system neither forgives nor forgets. Certainly the computer can be set to program out needless derogatory and confidential information; however, it has the capability to program this same information in. Should an unscrupulous person or even a well-meaning but overzealous government official wish to, he can delve behind the statistics to the inner secrets of an individual. Dr. Robert Morrison, scientific director of the Rockefeller Foundation, warned, "We are coming to recognize that organized knowledge puts an immense amount of power in the hands of the people who take the trouble to master it."[11]

The evolution of computerized data centers without effective public participation and protest can have a serious impact on our democratic process. Under our present system, individuals are expected to make fundamental choices where the future welfare is at stake, as would be the case in an election. By alienating the people from the decision-making process, control of the computer technology is left in the exclusive hands of those in possession of organizational power.

Vance Packard wrote that "the filekeepers of Washington have derogatory information of one sort or another on literally millions of people. The more files are fed into the central files, the greater the hazard the information will become enormously tempting to use as a form of control."[12]

Information in federal agencies is legally protected against improper use. The pooling, however, would create a different end-product, and power for the administrator of a computerized data bank. "It would appear obvious," according to Gallagher, "that the Federal official who has the authority to press the button to produce a dossier on any individual in the United States would possess a power greater than any ever before known in America."[13]

The Wall Street Journal, August 5, 1966, stated, "We do not suggest that many officials would attempt to abuse the power. Yet the fact is that even as it is, Federal agencies have been known to harass individuals or businesses, just as some of them have not been above electronic prying and other violations of privacy."[14]

Since the beginning of the Eisenhower Administration, individual tax information has been reviewed by several Congressional investigation groups on a "need-to-know basis." In the fall of 1967, President Johnson issued Executive Order 11383 headed "Inspection of Tax Returns,"[15] giving the Senate Ethics Committee the authority to inspect individual tax returns filed since 1948 by any Senator or Senate employee under investigation.

The order, in part, reads: ". . . any income, excess-profits, estate or gift tax return for the years 1948 to 1968 inclusive . . . in connection with its investigation of allegations that members, officers or employees of the Senate have engaged in improper conduct, or violated the rules and regulations of the Senate . . ."

Can we expect additional executive orders, next for members of Congress, later for all federal employees, and so on? When we all become the exception as a result of a "need-to-know" or "Executive Order," then public cooperation and faith in the entire tax system is threatened.

Originally, when an agency structured a confidential system to collect data, it was understood that the confidentiality would be permanently protected. This assurance, for example that a tax return is protected from a curious eye, is of major importance to us as we give evidence to the Internal Revenue Service on exactly how our income was achieved.

This confidence has recently been challenged. If we were told that tomorrow some federal subcommittee was going to review our returns over the past twenty years, we would quite naturally be upset; not necessarily from the need to hide anything, but rather from the failure of the illusion that our tax returns are confidential information.

In addition, there is the pressing question of accuracy of data. One possibility is suggested by Arthur R. Miller, a professor of law at the University of Michigan: Suppose you had exchanged Christmas cards with someone who was, unknown to you, a criminal, and whose mail was monitored by local security forces. It would come as quite a shock to find the index in your file, "Associates with known criminals."

The interpretation of behavior is a very complex matter. "The question of context is most graphically illustrated by the unexplained and incomplete arrest record. It is unlikely that a citizen whose file contains an entry 'arrested, 6/1/42; convicted felony, 1/6/43; three years, federal penitentiary' would be given federal employment or be accorded the governmental courtesies accorded other citizens. Yet the subject may simply have been a conscientious objector. And what about the entry 'arrested, disorderly conduct; sentenced six months Gotham City jail.' Without further explanation, who would know that

the person involved was a civil-rights demonstrator whose
conviction was reversed on appeal."[16]

Herman Kahn and Anthony Wiener, of the Hudson Institute,
a "think tank," wrote a book called *The Year 2000*, in which
they point out:

> Criteria for decisions are often too narrow because the
> decision-makers are parochial, partisan, or self-interested,
> or simply not accustomed to considering the new criteria
> that are becoming relevant. These new criteria are disre-
> garded simply because they are new; they were not con-
> sidered in the past so it is not reasonable that they should
> be considered now. If, for example, the Internal Revenue
> Service decides, in the interest of efficiency, to place very
> large amounts of personal information into computers, or
> the government, in the interests of science and efficiency,
> decides to centralize the records of twenty or more federal
> agencies in a National Data Bank, there is no existing
> pressure group (with the possible exception of Congress
> or the courts) organized to sound effective warnings of
> the dangers. If later, in the interests of law enforcement,
> this information is made widely available to other agen-
> cies, or even later, in the interest of commercial efficiency,
> the information is made available under "suitable" guard
> to credit groups, the final consequence may be an enor-
> mous invasion of privacy. Yet the people who value pri-
> vacy would not have had an effective chance to "vote"
> except in a perfunctory hearing or two, or perhaps by
> means of an *amicus curiae* brief filed by the ACLU
> (American Civil Liberties Union) if any test cases are
> fought. Presumably the democratic process provides many
> opportunities to affect such developments. Yet often
> enough the appropriate pressure group does not exist in
> an organized form effectively able to resist the groups that
> support the innovation. Even the constitutionality of an
> innovation may be difficult to test; the injured parties may
> not have "standing" insofar as they do not know or cannot
> prove how personal harm was done to them or indeed
> injured parties may exist only *in potentia*.[17]

The Federal Communications Commission, when it was planning an inquiry on the relationship between computers and communication services, stated on the problem of information privacy:

> . . . In the past, the invasion of information privacy was rendered difficult by the scattered and random nature of individual data. Now the fragmentary nature of information is becoming a relic of the past. Data centers and common memory drums housing competitive sales, inventory and credit information and untold amounts of personal information, are becoming common. This personal and proprietary information must remain free from unauthorized invasion or disclosure, whether at the computer, the terminal station, or the interconnecting communication link.[18]

Some federal agencies and their representatives are becoming concerned about the proposal for a national data bank. The public itself should question the drift of these techniques and tendencies. We should want to make certain that human dignity and civil liberties remain intact. We should demand to know the precise nature of the information that will be stored and who will have access to it. The public has the right to know who will have the power to control the computers and most importantly, how confidentiality and individual privacy can and will be protected.

Liberty is never gained once and for all. It is forever in conflict with civilization—a conflict which has no clear-cut solution but which reappears in cycles, usually in different forms. Each succeeding generation must win it anew. Each must defend it against ensuing dangers. This is necessary because we are continually changing our life environment; society may be altered so frequently that safeguards that in the past adequately protected our liberties become obsolete.

Science and technology are of immense benefit to society. They are so important to us that we would not want under most circumstances to impede their movement in advancing our knowledge of the world. But they may also expose our environment to great potential danger. Unless certain practices in the technological exploitation of scientific knowledge are restrained by law, they will cost us our liberties.

And we must constantly evaluate these technologies which are tools developed to increase man's power to understand his world; the mere fact that an innovation presents itself does not mean that we should surrender years of experience and values to its authority. Man alone bears the responsibility for the way he employs technological inventions. Yet it is difficult to bring social pressures to bear against the control of these dangerous technologies. One reason is that those who have the use of the technology are influential enough to prevent societal or, for that matter, legal restraints.

Chairman Gallagher, in the Congressional Record, reminds us that "Society borders on forgetting that technology is its own creation, to be guided and directed along the course which will provide its members most with the full benefits of scientific knowledge. The people seem dangerously prepared to surrender the age-old respect for the vast capabilities of the human mind and personality to the impressive and sometimes overwhelming knowledge which the scientific elite alone have mastered. Somewhat intimidated by the mystery of science, the average citizen in our Nation often seems reconciled to the sacrifice of individual liberties in the awesome name of 'progress.' "[19]

As computers become more dominant in our lives, we cannot for a moment afford to forget that a free society evolves around man and his actions. It is concerned with people's rights, interests and needs. Professor Lynn White, Jr., of the University of California, questions, "Must the miracle of the person succumb to the order of the computer?"[20] Our society ceases to be free when the dominant focus of life becomes the technology instead of the individual. If we let this happen we will have thrown away what we have so long fought for with sweat and blood. There is no law of nature that can guarantee us our human liberty or privacy—it is left to man to decide that condition of life.

According to Congressman Benjamin Rosenthal, who approached the Gallagher inquiry with initial skepticism, the projected national data center is an appropriate example of how technological innovation progresses at the expense of personal liberty. Rosenthal found it hardest to believe that the improved efficiency afforded by such a center would outweigh the clear risks. He posed several philosophic questions:[21] Is the threat to personal liberty too great a price to pay for the anticipated efficiency and progress? Are we sacrificing too many aspects of our personal lives for limited objectives? Does the additional knowledge we might gain yield benefits to society greater than the losses to the individual?

Jerome Wiesner, dean of science at M.I.T. and former science adviser to President Kennedy, cautioned us about the impact of rapid change:

> The computer, with its promise of a million fold increase in man's capacity to handle information, will undoubtedly have the most far-reaching social consequences of any contemporary technical development. The potential for good in the computer, and the danger inherent in its misuse, exceed our ability to imagine. . . . We have actually entered a new era of evolutionary history, one in which rapid change is a dominant consequence. Our only hope is to understand the forces at work and to take advantage of the knowledge we find to guide the evolutionary process.[22]

There seem to be a number of hazards in the growing fascination of the government's electronic file keepers with the idea of exchanging and pooling data on the lives of our citizens. First, using a central data bank to make decisions involving citizens encourages depersonalization. People increasingly resent being treated as numbers controlled by a computer. One sign of this is the student unrest on many college campuses. Second, a bank of this magnitude poses the potential hazard of increasing the citizens' distrust of their own government and alienating them from it. People resent telling their government anything when they discover that what they are confiding for one purpose may be used in some entirely different connection. A third hazard is that the bank will greatly increase the likelihood that the life chances of many citizens will be unfairly affected. A central file can absorb large batches of data about people, but it is ill-equipped to correct errors, allow for extenuating circumstances, or bring facts up to date. Computerized files, indifferent to the passage of time, would preserve data out of all proportion or relevance. Will the computer users have the capacity to recognize that people indeed often do change and become more responsible as they grow older? Finally, there is the hazard of permitting so much power to rest in the hands of those who push the computer buttons. When the details of our lives are fed into the central processor, where they are easily retrieved, we all fall to some extent under the control of the machine's managers.

For example, what control did the 6,400,000 New York State vehicle owners have when their names and addresses were sold to a marketing service, netting the state $86,000? In all probability, other business concerns will purchase this list from the marketing organization and our mailboxes will soon be flooded with new forms of advertising promotions.

Where does the power lie? Another data bank advance was made in 1968 when a centralized computer system called LOGIC (Local Government Information Control) was initiated for the one million residents in Santa Clara County, California. Included in this alphabetic index record are data such as name, alias, address, record of birth, driver's license, Social Security number, position if employed by county, property holdings, voter and jury status.

According to H. Taylor Buckner, a sociology professor at San Francisco State College, a National Computer Center is already in operation in Martinsburg, West Virginia. Taxpayers' records are stored there according to Social Security number and are compared with data provided by companies and banks. It is obvious that the day is not too far away when our Social Security number will become the primary source of contact within a national identity file.

Buckner voiced the following concern: "I see no reason to assume that the government will be any more resistant to the pressures of the moment in the future than it has been in the

past. Sending Japanese-American citizens to concentration camps would have been immensely speeded by having a National Identity and Data File, and McCarthy could have destroyed many more careers if he'd had computer records of security investigations. Protestors of current Viet Nam policy could easily be marked 'politically unreliable' for shipment off to the Tulelake Relocation Center after we bomb China."[23]
One great problem is that the availability of so large an information base would permit unscrupulous persons to use it for unlawful activities. We must be aware that modern organized crime has both the financial resources and access to the skills necessary to acquire and misuse the information in some of the systems now being considered. We must realize that not only can simple "automated blackmail machines" be created, but that data techniques, when fully defined, could draw chains of relationships from any person, organization or event to any other person, organization or event.

Paul Baran, of the Computer Sciences Department of the RAND Corporation, highlights a possible danger during election time: "The use of private detectives to unearth derogatory information on political candidates and their associates has become an increasingly prevalent feature of elections. This practice is expected to increase in the future. The cost per unit [of the] dirt mined by automated human garbage collectors can be cut by order of magnitude once they obtain access to a set of wide-access information systems which we now see being developed."[24]

To all this the director of the Washington office of the American Civil Liberties Union, Lawrence Speiser, responds: "Here is the crux of the matter. Unless and until a specific proposal is made which spells out what the national data center will collect, and hold, and what specific safeguards will be built in, it is our belief that Congress, representing the people, must insist that no affirmative action be taken toward this end."[25]

"There is a widespread belief," according to Baran in his 1965 book, "that somehow the communications network used will possess a God-given sanctuary to privacy, but 'it ain't necessarily so!' . . ."[26] In time there would be few areas left

in which an individual could move about in anonymity. There
would be few events in our lives that could not be fully
documented for future examination. Senator Edward V. Long
of Missouri claimed: "Society is continually pushing in on the
individual. He has only a few areas in which he can be himself, free from external restraint or observation."[27]

Man in American society must be provided with the right
to differ from others, and provided, too, with the right to
turn away from childhood shenanigans. He must be allowed
the errors and minor sins that are part of his life. He must
have the right to begin anew.

The rush to mechanize our entire record-apparatus is appalling. "I shall argue here the proposition that the regulation
of technology is the most important intellectual and political
task on the American agenda," claims W. H. Ferry, vice-
president of the Fund for the Republic. "The first point to be
made is that technology can no longer be taken for granted.
It must be thought about, not merely produced, celebrated,
and accepted in all its manifestations as an irrepressible and
essentially benign human phenomenon." Referring to the per-
sistent pressure of modern-day technology, Ferry states: "My
first example is privacy, today a goner, killed by technology."[28]

The greatest fear is that computerized banks have perfect
memory, which guarantees that their records could follow a
man throughout his life. In its final report to Congress, the
subcommittee's chairman voiced his concern that modern
computer technology will attempt "to establish on the basis
of compiled data on man's past actions axiomatic principles
for predicting what he will do in the future—and that these
principles will become accepted by society as nearly infallible.
The final result would be the restriction of man's future based
upon the statistical pattern of his actions in his youth."[29]

The issue before 200 million Americans is not whether a
statistical data bank can be established or whether it would
in any way be beneficial. The central concern is that an im-
balance is threatened among the potentials of our future
technologies, the law and the public interest. The issue is
whether we can achieve a balance that will assure that technological progress will serve us and that man's freedom will

dominate in the new environment that the computer is rapidly bringing about. The Big Brother of 1984 may not be a greedy power-seeker, but rather a relentless bureaucrat or opportunist obsessed with efficiency, who may use information for purposes other than those for which it was collected. According to Edward Shils in his discussion of privacy and power:

> It seems to me that once an institution like a National Data Center became established it would be a perpetual source of trouble. For one thing its administration would acquire a professional vested interest in the satisfaction of their cognitive appetite. As long as computers could cope or could be designed to cope with such quantities of material, there would be what would sound like good and reasonable arguments for making the informational archives of the government complete. On the outside, it would be a perpetual excitement and temptation to the professional breachers of privacy and the exploiters of such breachers. Journalists would demand access on behalf of the public interest, so would legislators. And private operatives might be able to bribe their way to information on particular persons.[30]

Today's college generation, in particular, is challenging the apparent complacency and indifference of its senior leadership. That privacy will forever remain because it is implied in the Constitution and the Bill of Rights is not credible to the new adult population. With growing hostility toward the dominating technology and the establishment, a segment of this group fear that the documentation of their so-called acts of rebellion will only show that the freedoms once assumed have been surrendered. Should our older citizens in power fail to come to grips with the issue of preservation of privacy, it can be expected that the last struggle will be made by those who question how their present behavior, if documented, could be used against them at some future time.

The computer cannot be blamed for loss of privacy. It is but an instrument created by man. Computers and other advanced machine systems are not permitted to be in error; but man is not a machine and does not have to be as efficient as the tools he has created to serve him. If man loses his right to be wrong, will he react by withdrawing from society? Will his curiosity to experiment with life falter? If this happens, man truly becomes nothing more than a machine.

CHAPTER II

The Proposed
National Data Bank

The stereotype of the government office, with secretaries
hidden behind piles of papers in triplicate, fails to convey
the enormous record keeping within the federal system.

Where do you put information on 200 million people? In
December, 1964, an inventory was made of punch cards and
computer tapes held by a variety of federal agencies. It was
found, for example, that the Bureau of the Census' population
figures alone are contained in an unrestricted file of 4,072
tapes and a confidential file of 7,297 tapes. The department's
annual survey of manufacturers contains a confidential file of
6,399,000 cards and 880 tapes. The Internal Revenue Service
has more than 2,500 tapes for reporting individual income
taxes over a period of three years.

Overall, the government figures are staggering. More than
100 million punch cards and 30,000 computer tapes are used
by just seven major federal departments to accumulate over
600 bodies of statistical data. By examining the capacity of
punch cards and tapes, one can get an idea of how much

data can be collected. A standard punch card contains 80 characters (letters or numbers), while a standard tape can hold in the neighborhood of 40 million characters. About 8 billion inputs on punch cards and a potential of more than 1,200 billion inputs on tapes are at the disposal of only seven government departments. This figure excludes papers and reports filed away in thousands of cabinets.

Every government has to collect and store information in order to function, but the magnitude of the task facing our own is due to more than our size and complexity. One of the difficulties in keeping records in the United States is that we have a highly decentralized governmental system. We have no central statistical office which is responsible for all the record keeping of the nation as many countries do. Instead, each of the large administrative and regulatory agencies within our system undertakes to provide much of the data it requires. For example, the Bureau of Labor Statistics collects information on wholesale and retail prices, wage rates, employment and a wide variety of other information relating to the role of labor in the economy. The Office of Business Economics provides data on the national income accounts, showing the progress of business activities and the functioning of the economy. The Federal Trade Commission and the Securities and Exchange Commission collect quarterly financial reports on manufacturing operations. The Department of Health, Education and Welfare collects the basic statistics on education and health.

In a great many instances, these statistics are a direct by-product of the federal regulatory process resulting from daily routine activities. The Internal Revenue Service processes personal and business income tax returns and provides tabulations which constitute a basic statistical source. The Social Security Administration has large bodies of information on wage and salary payments to individuals. However, one federal agency, the Bureau of the Census, performs many of the functions normally undertaken by a central statistical office. It is responsible for comprehensive data on population, housing, agriculture, manufacturers, retail and wholesale trade, transportation and government bodies.

The Office of Statistical Standards of the Bureau of the

Budget has the function of improving, developing, and coordinating federal statistical services. All survey forms which are set out by federal agencies for the collection of data must have the approval of the Office of Statistical Standards. Since it is a unit of the Bureau of the Budget, it participates in the review of budget requests of the various agencies for statistical activities.

Feeding into this process is the National Archives and Records Service. It has responsibility for promoting improved current records, management, and disposal practices of federal agencies. In addition, it selects, preserves and makes available to the government and public the permanently valuable non-current records of the federal government. The National Archives holds in warehouses the tax returns filed by corporations since 1909.

The computer is not new to the federal government. The Bureau of the Census acquired the first Univac in 1952. In fact, the federal government is the biggest purchaser of computers in the country. One half of all computers sold go to the government and it is anticipated that over $2 billion will be spent on computers in 1970. Forty-five computers were in government use in 1954, rising to 1,770 in a ten-year period. The total has gone from 1,946 systems in 1965 to 2,600 in 1967. There are at least 5,000 people about the capital who do nothing but sell, coordinate and maintain computers for the government, and more than 75,000 people who operate them.

Federal agencies have rapidly learned the advantages of mechanizing their routines. By now the technological innovation of computer systems is an integral and essential arm of the federal government. It has increased efficiency and substantially reduced the amount of time and labor required in data processing. In the processing of the 1960 population, the time required for certain steps was reduced from several years to several months.

Utilization of computers in government operations has also made possible new kinds of analysis. It is possible to examine and edit much more carefully. In the case of census data for manufacturing establishments, the computer can spot errors in reporting wage bills and man-hours by computing average hourly earnings. For some agencies, the ability of the computer to make consistency checks is also very important. Thus the Internal Revenue Service uses computers to check the internal consistency of items contained in each individual tax form.

Until the computer was used, information had to be reduced and simplified to make it more manageable in solving problems. Now it is possible to use all the same basic data many times over in different types of analysis. In addition, computers have made possible new types of analysis. Collected tabulations of individual tax returns used to be employed to estimate the impact proposed tax law changes might have on total tax revenue and on particular classes of taxpayers. The computer has made this analysis more reliable. This was demonstrated by recomputing 100,000 tax returns individually according to the proposed revision in the law. This provided a cumulative measurement of total revenue, and permitted an analysis of which classes of taxpayers would be affected, and to what extent.

The power of the computer to handle and interrelate large masses of information has encouraged different agencies in the federal system to bring together data which they collect on related economic units. A by-product of interagency cooperation to make data analysis more efficient has been an improvement in the standardization of classification systems, techniques and methodology. In order to collate data from different sources, federal agencies use identical classification systems and treat similar cases in a uniform manner. Information required as a basis for major legislative and executive policy decisions must draw on many kinds of data.

A totally integrated computer system would increase the ability of various federal agencies to coordinate their basic data and would provide more reliable information for policy purposes.

Already some major high-level services are being provided. According to John Macy of the Civil Service Commission:

> These systems will mesh well with developing plans for an executive level staffing program which will be designed to locate the best possible man for any given top-level assignment, no matter where in Government he

may be serving. The computer's ability to search its perfect memory and pick out records of individuals with specific characteristics has been applied in the search for candidates for Presidential appointments. . . . A computerized file containing the names and employment data of some 25,000 persons all considered likely prospects for Federal appointive positions, is searched electronically. . . . This telebank, with its automated retrieval system, broadens the field of consideration for the President in critical decisions of leadership selection.[1]

One of the models used in developing a proposal for a federal data center is the Manpower Information System. Initiated several years ago by the Bureau of Labor Statistics of the Department of Labor, it is a system for the storage, retrieval and analysis of the nation's major collection of employment and unemployment information.

The data is received in two ways. From a series of monthly interviews by the Census Bureau of a sample of 35,000 households, information is provided on occupation, race, marital status, age, employment status, level of skill and other demographic data. The second source is monthly historical data for about 350 industries on hours of work, hourly and weekly earnings, number employed and labor turnover.

In addition to this information and that received from states and cities, over 12 million monthly reports were submitted by 170,000 business organizations since 1957, and placed on magnetic tapes. Systematically arranged in files by establishment, month and industry, these tapes are available for different forms of analysis relating to the business cycle and other economic and social considerations. This data system has proved useful to the Department of Labor, other agencies, and qualified institutional researchers.

A parallel effort, started in September, 1965, is the National Crime Information Center of the Federal Bureau of Investigation. Through this information network encompassing the entire country, data can be made available to law enforcement agencies in seconds. This system does not just contain information from FBI files, but is also tied in with local metropolitan and state-wide networks. At the outset, the center included data on 168,006 stolen cars; 45,306 license plates; 88,022 stolen properties; and 20,367 wanted persons. High-speed computers permit rapid communication. In January, 1967, the center was put into operation with several local systems. The FBI believes that with this new approach, "instant information" on current situations will become a reality for the investigator and the officer on the street. Although the NCI Center is presently narrow in scope, future plans call for expanding it to collect much more intelligence data. What safeguards will control the FBI operation is a question still to be asked.

Additional insights may be gained from studying the New York State Identification and Intelligence System, which has placed in its computer 540,000 of its 6 million fingerprint records and data on associates of crime-syndicate figures.

The initial interest in a national computerized data center can be traced to a convention held in 1959. In December of that year the American Economic Association devoted part of its meeting to consideration of the preservation and use of data for economic research. Although they believed it was important, they concluded that it would be difficult for their organization to develop a large system. Therefore the association recommended that the Social Science Research Council, a non-profit institution, start a feasibility survey, which it did in December, 1960.

A committee was set up to explore problems in the field of economic data alone. It was composed of people acquainted with statistical work being done in the federal government. The chairman was Richard Ruggles of the Yale University Department of Economics. In order to make their efforts most effective, they chose to concentrate on those areas which would yield the most valuable research materials per unit of cost. This meant excluding from consideration information too widely scattered throughout the government or stored in warehouses. The committee urged that attention be focused on those bodies of information currently available in machine-readable form.

An agency-by-agency study was made during the three-year

period from 1962 through 1964. Meetings were arranged with a considerable number of independent agencies in the U.S. Departments of Commerce, Labor, Treasury, Agriculture, Interior and Health, Education, and Welfare. In addition, the committee kept in close contact with the Bureau of the Budget and the National Archives.

Now that dramatically large volumes of data could be economically stored and conveniently retrieved, the important question was what should be preserved. The committee recommended establishing a group to review regularly important data produced by federal agencies or subcommittees, and to develop procedures for insuring the adequate preservation of such data.

The problem of access to information became a dominant one for the Ruggles' committee. At their suggestion, the Bureau of the Budget and the National Archives jointly undertook a survey in December, 1964, of machine-readable data held by various government agencies. The preliminary survey covered some twenty agencies, including units of the Departments of Agriculture, Commerce, Labor, Treasury and Health, Education, and Welfare, resulting in over 600 major bodies of data listed. The data were stored on approximately 100 million punch cards and 30,000 computer tapes. Not all of this data is usable. Different agencies employ different techniques. Federal agencies do not always provide clean, edited tapes or supporting information about the data.

The Ruggles committee also discussed the problems inherent in disclosure. They reported that a considerable portion of the information collected from individuals and businesses is obtained with the understanding that it will be considered confidential. For example, in the case of the Annual Survey of Manufacturers, the data on the activities of manufacturing establishments constitute a confidential report to the Bureau of the Census and are protected by law from use by such agencies as the Internal Revenue Service for the purpose of checking tax returns, or even by Congress in its various investigating functions.

It is recognized by all concerned that federal agencies should not violate the confidentiality of their data by making them available to outside research workers or other agencies.

However, it is often possible to disguise information so that it cannot be traced specifically to an individual respondent. In the last few years the Bureau of the Census has made available a sample of information on 100,000 individual households that gives a considerable amount of detail about the age, education, income, occupation, and so forth of the individuals in the household. The omission of detailed geographic information makes it impossible to trace the data to any specific individual.

In the spring of 1967 a departure was made from the traditional census taken by the federal government. A hundred and twenty thousand households in New Haven, Connecticut, and ten surrounding towns received trial questionnaires from the Bureau of the Census. One-fourth of the people surveyed, instead of being asked the basic 14 questions, were asked to respond to 118 questions, many of them new. Among these questions were:

What is your Social Security number?

What were you doing five years ago—working? military service? keeping house? attending school? something else?

Did you earn a college degree, and if so in what field?

Did you complete a vocational, business or technical training program?

Are such items as heat, electricity, air conditioning and a swimming pool included in the rent you pay?

Does your home have a garbage disposal unit? a color TV set? a dishwasher?

The 1970 census will sample the population with new questions such as, How often have you been married? Do you own more than one home? Is anyone in your household physically disabled in any way? Refusal to release this information to the census taker can lead to a fine of $100 or 30 days in jail.

The Internal Revenue Service developed a sample of 100,000 personal income tax returns that could not be traced to any particular individual. With other types of data the problem is more difficult. For example, the mere indication of the size and industry of a manufacturing plant may be sufficient to identify it.

In a striking statement, Representative Frank Horton claimed that the attraction of a federal data center lies in the area of getting sophisticated automated techniques to keep abreast of what large corporations are doing.

The Ruggles committee concluded that ". . . because of the decentralized nature of the federal statistical system and the pressure of the primary functions of the agencies, neither outside scholars nor Federal agencies are able to utilize efficiently the large amount of information which has been obtained at public expense."[2] Therefore, the committee urged that a federal data center be established by the federal government. Its purpose would be to preserve and make available to both government and nongovernment users basic statistical data that originated in all federal agencies.

According to Raymond T. Bowman, Assistant Director for Statistical Standards, Bureau of the Budget, the major reasons for the establishment of a federal statistical data center would be to bring all available statistical information to bear on problems which confront the nation, and to reduce the length of questionnaires.

For this to be workable, the center would have to have authority to obtain computer tapes from other federal agencies. Since duplication of computer tape is relatively inexpensive, a clean, edited tape could be housed with the originating agency and a copy with the federal data center. In addition, all statistical projects within the federal domain would include a budget item for the preparation of tapes.

Congressman Gallagher raised several pertinent questions on making the varying agency tapes useful in a central data center. When transporting the tapes what safeguards would be taken to guard against bugging; to protect against interception; and to exercise control over who will program the information? The questions of who will have the key and who will mind the tapes have to be considered.

In order to discharge its responsibility, the federal data center would require substantial computer capability. It would not only furnish basic information, but also, on a reimbursable basis, itself make production runs and furnish collected tapes or results to scholars so as to eliminate many problems of disclosure. In a great many instances, the proposal continues, the center would find it advisable to develop new tapes that combine information from different federal agencies.

The center would also act as a servicing facility, providing specific information directly to federal agencies and individuals and publishing descriptions of data. Serving somewhat the same function as the Library of Congress, it would insure that the most useful information was preserved in usable form, and that duplicative and unwanted data did not clog the system. The center would provide basic information about the American economy as a primary objective rather than as a by-product of the administrative or regulatory function.

Since the Bureau of the Budget had had the responsibility of developing programs and issuing regulations for the improved gathering, compiling, analyzing, publishing, and disseminating of statistical information, the committee urged that this bureau take the necessary steps to establish a federal data center.

A major incentive for adopting this proposal for a center of economic data was that it would be used by scholars and researchers. A plan of strategy suggested by Ruggles' committee was that the Social Science Research Council gather representatives from research institutions and universities currently engaged in research projects using empirical information. This group would consider: (1) how the research interests of all nonprofit research organizations and universities could be promoted; (2) what kinds of services could be provided for these organizations; (3) what kinds of coordination would be desirable; (4) how the center of economic data would be established, staffed and financed; (5) in what ways the proposed center could assist the federal government in the establishment of a federal data center; and (6) in what way this organization could advise the federal government on development and preservation of basic data.

In the spring of 1965 the Ruggles committee submitted its report to the Social Science Research Council. The Office of Statistical Standards engaged Edgar S. Dunn, Jr., a research analyst at Resources for the Future, Inc., to serve as a consultant to the Bureau of the Budget. His final report was submitted on November 1, 1965.

With reference to the Ruggles report, Dunn said:

> The Ruggles Committee report gave us a healthy beginning toward an evaluation of this problem in realistic terms. However, this group did not have the time or staff resources to spell out the total problem set in a way that seems essential to support a more detailed consideration of program options. There is also a tendency in this report to see the problem primarily in terms of the accessibility of existing records and the solution in terms of the extension of user services. There is much that is valid in this representation but it gives insufficient attention to the important fact that accessibility is bound up with all of the production procedures and is inseparable in a number of fundamental respects from the issues related to the quality and scope of the existing records. It seems useful, therefore, to attempt a more precise formulation of the problem set to the solution of which the data center concept is addressed.[3]

The Dunn report analyzed what had been some of the systemic deficiencies in the combined federal statistical effort. With computers, he noted, new statistical tools that had never been feasible before could be used for public policy analysis.

Dunn suggested that "the concept of a National Data Center is an appropriate vehicle for program reform if the concept is broadened to emphasize the role of the servicing capability and if it can be given an important role in assisting the Bureau of the Budget to establish standards and monitor compliance. Accordingly the basic recommendation is for the establishment of a National Data Service Center." It would be responsible for:

1. File storage and management of significant archival records.
2. A central referral and reference source for the users of federal statistics.

3. Explicit facilitating services for the users of federal data such as file rearrangement, tape translation, record matching, disclosure by-passing, and performance of standard statistical routines.
4. Development of computer hardware and software systems.
5. Provision of staff support to work in conjunction with the Bureau of the Budget to develop and establish standards essential to the system capability.[4]

Raymond Bowman, the Assistant Director for Statistical Standards, Bureau of the Budget, argues that a data center would improve our access to information for statistical purposes and should be organized to maintain confidentiality of those individuals who supply data. When statistics are used to test a thesis, it is not necessary that they identify individuals, and therefore the center would not keep individual dossiers. He insists that the information in the files of the center would be prohibited for any purpose other than statistical.

The White House appointed a special task force headed by Dr. Carl Kaysen, an economist who had served with the Kennedy Administration and is now chairman of the Institute for Advanced Study at Princeton. The Kaysen Report, as it was later called, unequivocally urged the establishment of a data center, and suggested it include data from state and local governments.[5] An example of improved efficiency would be the relating of employment figures now isolated within the Department of Labor to the Federal Reserve's data on individual production.

Later, however, in testimony before the Senate Subcommittee on Administrative Practice and Procedure, Kaysen said: "Well, I am not trying to say that the system is totally safe against cracking. I do not think you can ever produce a system that is totally proof against cracking."[6]

One of the arguments about the federal data bank concerns the differences between a statistical and an informational storage system. The defenders of the center claim that it would be a statistical system, in contrast with an informational system which generates intelligence about individuals. Informational systems are widely used and considered essential by private and public businesses. These systems include data about such things as doctors' medical records and teachers' educational records; they include data that are essential to public administration—licensing authorities' information on whether a driver has legal vision, or requirements for the administration of taxes.

According to Dunn, there are two ways that a statistical system can be prevented from turning into an intelligence system: statutory and other legal restrictions that prohibit release of individual data, and protections stemming from the technical design of the system. As an example of the latter, Dunn remarks that a computer tape can't be read by the layman. It requires a machine, a codebook, an appropriate set of instructions and a technician.

But some are dubious. Disillusionment was expressed by Arthur R. Miller:

> First, if all the information gathered about an individual is in one place, the payoff for snooping is sharply enhanced. Thus, although the cost or difficulty of gaining access may be great, the amount of dirt available once access is gained is also great. Second, there is every reason to believe that the art of electronic surveillance will continue to become more efficient and economical. Third, governmental snooping is rarely deterred by cost.
> . . . Any increase in the amount of recorded information is certain to increase the risk of errors in reporting and recording and indexing. Information distortion also will be caused by machine malfunctioning. Moreover, people working with the data in Washington or at a distance through remote terminals can misuse the information. . . . Our success or failure in life ultimately may turn on what other people decide to put into our files and on the programmer's ability, or inability, to evaluate, process, and interrelate information. The great bulk of the information likely to find its way into the center will be gathered and processed by relatively unskilled and unimaginative people who lack discrimination and sensitivity.[7]

Paul Baran, the computer expert quoted here in Chapter One, also feels that the line between statistical and intelligence systems is fuzzy. If one wants to extract intelligence information from a statistical system he can; and, as well, statistical information can be extracted from an intelligence system. The major difference is that it would be a little easier to use the machine for one purpose than the other, but this does not deny the exchangeability of information. Trained intelligence personnel could derive potentially damaging data even from a statistical system. Burton E. Squires, Jr., Assistant Professor of Computer Sciences at Pennsylvania State University claims that what is called a statistical data center and what is called an intelligence data center do not differ in the kind of information they store.

Finally, Lawrence Speiser of the American Civil Liberties Union says: "Proponents of the bank have to date stressed that the bank is limited to statistical data, not of the kind that would lend itself to the building of a dossier. We have great doubt that information contained in the files of some 20-odd federal agencies that would be placed in the bank, even if it were called statistical, would not contain much that is indeed of a highly personal nature that could be harmful in the ways we are talking about."[8] To date, this remains an open and debatable issue.

On the basis of the data included in a sample archive, it was estimated that a more complete archive would include about 20,000 reels of magnetic tape, cost a total of $3 to $3.5 million and take 3 to 5 years to develop. Of this amount $800,000 would be needed to bring data not now machine-accessible into usable form, about $500,000 would be needed to transfer punched card data to magnetic tape. In addition, between $500,000 and $1 million would be essential for blank reels and tape copying.

Almost half of this file, 9,000 reels, could be brought into a data center for about $260,000 within a year. This indicates that the files vary widely in the quality of their maintenance and documentation. Bringing the remaining half in would cost about $300 a reel compared with $37 a reel for the first 9,000 reels. Added to this are the storage costs: less than $10,000 annually for 20,000 reels in prime air-conditioned space. Consequently, a totally taped program of the type outlined under the recommendations would probably start out with an expenditure of $1 or $2 million in the first year and grow to the neighborhood of at least $10 million annually.

This, of course, is a relatively small sum. It does not include the cost of building a center and fitting it with the appropriate computer hardware; however, even with this expenditure the monies needed to put the federal data bank into operation would be minor. Compared to our defense spending, the installation of a bank would hardly be noticeable on the balance sheet. To some taxpayers the reaction will be "go ahead, it really doesn't cost that much." For some Congressmen, regardless of their own feelings about the data center, the reaction will be similar: "Why not, it doesn't really affect our budget—let's try it on an experimental basis." The fact that the center would be inexpensive might become an important incentive in getting it approved. Cost should be an administrative question asked only after the more crucial question of whether we should have a federal data center at all.

Specialists at the National Bureau of Standards have also expressed support of a federal data center because of the services it could offer. It could provide data in cases where the primary agency possessing the data is not capable of making them available in the required format, detail, flexibility or quality. Primary agencies would continue to provide data which they can furnish in the needed form, even though they had previously delivered the relevant basic data to the center. For example, an agency might produce statistics as a by-product of its principal mission, having no resources to organize the information for flexible or rapid access. Or the data might require adjustment or reconciliation which the collecting agency cannot perform as well as the center can.

In addition, the center would provide data in those cases where the information originates in two or more reporting systems or agencies. This would make information about interrelationships available in maximum feasible detail, without restrictions resulting from screening for improper disclosures at the time of transfer into the center. The central bank would also maintain an archive of statistical data, with all corrections and adjustments made consistently and accompanied by code-books and manuals.

Responses to queries or outputs would be provided in a variety of forms at the customer's option—printed tabulations, machine-readable tapes, graphs, diagrams, etc.—either locally or through telecommunications.

The federal statistical data center would establish, keep up to date, and operate a reference and referral service for federal statistical operations. This service would not concern itself with the actual provision of data, but would deal more with matters that a user might need before he can formulate a proper query. The reference and referral center would give information about various concepts that lie behind the statistics: general imports in contrast with imports for consumption; total employment and number of employees in specific establishments; industry and product statistics and so forth.

Automatic data-processing equipment would also be available for computation and data reduction in response to queries of customers; it would provide cross tabulations, averages, distribution statistics, smoothed curves, trend fittings, seasonal adjustments, periodic analyses, correlations, regressions, and more advanced analyses in order to give access to the full range of information computable from the collection. Confidential audits would be performed by machine upon the information intended for release to customers.

Computer equipment would also support a battery of services of the federal government. It would be able to make statistical data more meaningful over a period of time. It would also detect errors in primary collections or derived statistics through consistency tests and detection routines. It would conduct computations and identify sources of error. With combinations of these computations it could run validation studies of the quality of federal statistics and add such techniques to existing appraisals.

According to Glaser, Rosenblatt and Wood, all of the National Bureau of Standards, four general principles emerge for constructing a federal statistical data center:[9]

> (1) Maximum ability to exhibit the interrelations among various kinds of data;

(2) The unification of all information about the individual reporting unit or analytical unit;

(3) The preservation of detail in the basic records and the avoidance of loss of information in the storage, manipulation and retrieval of information; and

(4) The ability to produce the full measure of inherent information which is computable from the basic records.

It is recognized by the National Bureau of Standards' experts that there are still complex and difficult issues which require intensive study. However, they believe these issues can be resolved with the aid of tools of the computer sciences.

In summary, the main purpose of a federal statistical data center is to create a better-integrated information network for use by government, industry and the research community. Its operation, hopefully, should lead to better-informed choices among alternative policies and programs and more effective program implementation.

:

This, then, is the proposal to consolidate some of the major federal filing systems into one vast central data bank. It would require that confidential information now in government files be forwarded to a new group and used for purposes other than those for which it was originally intended. It would also require that a new group have the code and access to the names, addresses, and backgrounds of the people to whom the data relate. At first this central storage center would pool information now in the files of twenty different federal agencies. Presumably in future years more and more agencies, along with more and more of their records, would enter this pool.

Civil Service Commission Chairman John Macy, in that now famous *Saturday Review* article, stated: "In forecasting manpower needs and important decisions of career planning, for proper decisions in these areas, we must have integrated information systems. This will require the use of information across departmental boundaries. It is here that current efforts to standardize symbols and codes will pay dividends. Direct tape-to-tape feeding of data from one department to another may become common."[10]

In the past, if there was a breakdown in the security of one agency, it did not necessarily mean a breakdown in another agency. With a central data bank, if there were a breakdown it would be a formidable problem that could undermine our entire economic and social system. In addition, errors could be made in the recording process when the data are converted from English into machine-readable form. What consequences would there be when a machine system breaks down or operates incorrectly leading to the possibility of data distortion? These problems in existing computerized systems will most certainly become more crucial with data centers.

A major issue is the possible misuse of the system by people who program the computer, by those who feed it the data on tapes and cards, by those who act as watchers of the memory unit, by those who actually work the computer and, when it is tied in to terminals across the country, by those who will be waiting for the data.

Should this proposal be accepted and put into practice in its present form, we will witness the evolution of an enormously efficient computerized system. The national data bank will serve us in many ways, providing our society with information that will increase our welfare as a group. It will undoubtedly eliminate a lot of waste and expand our opportunities for more precise planning and decision-making.

Yet, in developing this powerful organization, a new type of secrecy seems to be the order of the day. The files are growing and computerized data banks are expanding, but there is little dialogue on how these events may be affecting our lives. Technicians and their followers are dedicated to the principle of advancement of technology and may fail to give sufficient attention to the social impact of their innovations. A larger segment of our population should share in determining the survival of our private world, our ability to be free from surveillance, and our struggle to stand clear of the all-seeing eye.

The crucial issue goes beyond whether or not we have a formally organized national data center. Even if there is no such centralized data repository, a threat to our privacy remains. What if the FBI has access to data in the Department of Health, Education and Welfare, or if the Internal Revenue Service transmits data to the Bureau of the Census? This kind of activity would mean the establishment in fact, if not in name, of a federal data bank.

CHAPTER III

The Keeper of Records: More Data Banks and Computer Installations

The collection, storage and retrieval techniques that would be found in a federal data bank are not unique. Data banks, and in particular computerized data banks, have been in use in industry, education and welfare institutions for more than a decade. However, once a federal center of such proportions is operational, it will serve as a model. The result will be more and more efficient repositories with improved storing, analyzing and retrieving approaches.

Not all computerized systems are data banks. Some operations merely act as accounting systems and high-speed calculators, while others at more sophisticated levels are depositories for internal decision-making; some store research information from diverse sources; and some are documentors for the purpose of assimilation and distribution of pertinent data to a larger community.

Not all data banks contain the "sensitive" or potentially "threatening" information that might be found in a federal data center. But the possibility of incorporating such information does exist. Even the rather elementary, antiquated computer has the potential for being an information storage center. It doesn't matter whether it is formally called a "bank" or a "single unit processor"—any capacity to collect, store and retrieve data instantaneously upon request may, if misused, infringe on personal privacy.

Automated Business— The Most Efficient Entrepreneur

As one example, Dun and Bradstreet has a sales and marketing identification service. A decade ago it adopted the government's Standard Industrial Classification Code and now has put its entire roster of U.S. manufacturing establishments on IBM magnetic tape systems. The result is a powerfully computerized file on 300,000 manufacturing organizations with a maximum of twenty marketing facts for each. As needed adjustments are reported by Dun and Bradstreet's field credit investigators, the dossier is immediately brought up to date. Information documented includes name, address, telephone number, name of chief executive, line of business, Standard Industrial Classification Code; figures on employees, sales, branches, etc., and net worth and credit rating for credit subscribers. Access to the "combination lock" can provide the finder with facts on nearly every profit-making organization in the country and, since some have foreign operations, facts on business around the world. Standard and Poor's subsidiary, Standard Statistics, has had a Compustat Service in operation in the area of security analysis. It houses pertinent financial information, dating from 1946, on leading industrial and utility companies in the United States. Information is updated ten to twelve times a year.

The American Stock Exchange has an "Am-Quote" which is a computerized telephone quotation service enabling member brokers and their customers to get faster, more reliable and comprehensive data at speeds up to 72,000 inquiries an hour on any of the 1,100 issues traded. And there is never a busy signal; private telephone lines are hooked up between a TeleCenter and regular desk telephones in a broker's office. Within two seconds of dialing, a recorded voice supplies the latest market information on the stock that the broker has asked about. The entire message is completed in merely twenty-five seconds.

The New York Stock Exchange announced in June 1968 plans to establish a computer-fed information center. It would set up an electronic clearing house to give data on the location of large blocks of listed stocks. When operational it should determine where stock is held and expressions of interest in trading; allow greater speed in obtaining bids; get order executions and receive reports back more efficiently. Preventing this information from getting into the wrong hands should be a primary concern. Dr. William C. Freund, vice-president of the New York Stock Exchange, voiced his anxiety: "All institutional data must be treated confidentially with the source of information exercising control."[1]

The commercial banking system, next to the federal government, is the largest consumer of paper. For example, in one year alone banks handled 15 billion checks. In the last six years check handling has been largely computerized so that over 90 per cent of the checks in circulation today are MICR (Magnetic Ink Character Recognition) coded. Nearly all banks have their own computers for check handling and other bank functions.

An unusual application is found at California's Bank of America. It offers to doctors and dentists a service whereby all charges and payments are reported each day over the telephone to the bank. The bank prepares the monthly statements on its computer, mails them to the patients, and sends accounting reports to the doctor or dentist. According to the Bank of America, this system reduces accounting and billing time in the medical office by about 80 per cent.

Computers are also central to the growing numbers of credit bureaus throughout the country. Dale L. Reistad, director of automation and marketing research for the American Banking Association, believes that city-wide universal credit-card systems will soon come into existence, and will be followed by a nation-wide credit system.

In all probability the most efficient file system in the country, outside of the government, is a conglomeration of more than 2,200 local credit bureaus. All but a hundred of these belong to the Associated Credit Bureaus of America and presently have information on about 110 million Americans.[2] More than seven million reports are exchanged annually among members. Their files may have data on: length of employment on present job; history of past positions; approximate monthly earnings; number of dependents; type of housing—rented or owned; estimate of bank savings; loans, mortgages, installment purchases and other debts and how they were paid; and any legal involvements and their outcome. Information in these files might show that a person has borrowed money to pay off a washing machine, two cars and some household furniture, and where relevant, might give some indication of how successful his marriage is.

In *Buy Now, Pay Later,*[3] Hillel Black claims that the Associated Credit Bureaus of America probably contain in their files more data on more persons than the CIA and FBI combined.

The Atlanta-based Retail Credit Company, with 1,800 offices throughout the continent, has records on more than 45 million people. About 40,000 of their users receive each year 35 million reports containing information ranging from family size to extramarital affairs and homosexuality.

The most disturbing feature is that credit bureaus, in contrast with federal agencies, are not regulated by the law. Instead, credit sellers mutually agree to keep data confidential by using a code number when requesting information. In addition to annual dues of $25 to $50, credit bureau members are charged fees by the parent organization for information on individuals. For example, the Credit Bureau of Greater New York—the largest of its kind in the nation—charges $.55 for file data on a person's habits of paying his bills as well as a check on his personal references; a check on his mortgage loan costs $4.50; and special reports are $10 plus expenses. Searches are done for organizations ranging from department stores to car-rental firms. Their files on 8.5 million people occupy the entire floor of an office building. About 780,000 "derogatory items" are added each year to these New York files. Some data relate to the nonpayment of bills and court decisions. Most of the information is obtained from court records.

Errors occur. A woman ordered a carpet for her home and received the correct rug but in the wrong color. The supplier refused to exchange it and when she said she wouldn't pay, sued her for the cost of the item. The case was dismissed but the woman's credit file now shows that she was sued for non-payment and her credit record was seriously damaged.

Once an error is made it is difficult to correct it. Chester J. Straub, a New York City lawyer and state assemblyman, said that he was rejected by a credit card organization because of a mistaken credit bureau report. "The entry indicated that a judgment was outstanding against me which in fact wasn't mine. It belonged to someone with a similar name."[4] Only after pointing out that he was an assemblyman, did he get the credit bureau to alter his files.

The New York Credit Bureau employs 500 people who have access to 8.5 million dossiers. But credit bureau members are not the only ones to utilize these files. The FBI and the State Department receive each year more than 20,000 of their reports.

Far-reaching as the system is at present, work is under way for developing a powerful nation-wide computerized center to further facilitate collection and distribution of credit data. The Associated Credit Bureaus of America is implementing a network of computerized banks that by 1972 will make possible instant access to credit records throughout the country. It should be remembered that in 1950, installment credit totaled nearly $15 billion. By early 1967 it was nearly $75 billion or about $375 for every person in this country.

A Los Angeles *Times* article described three recently installed credit-reporting computers that "together will keep tabs on the bill-paying habits of millions of people throughout the Southwest and in New York."[5] One system in New York City will commence with "some 17 million persons in New York." Another installation, utilizing television-type displays, will picture "the entire credit file of an individual."

Insurance company files are growing too. There is an enormous central file of nearly 17 million records maintained by the insurance industry and utilized by companies throughout the country. The Hooper-Holmes Bureau of Morristown, New Jersey, has amassed a claims file of more than 6.5 million persons. In the case of insurance, the leakage of data may be more damaging than that of legal and money matters held by credit bureaus. These insurance organizations seek out those who might be called "moral hazards," persons whose behavior might lead to violence or death. In fact, some insurance firms won't write policies for people they believe to be homosexuals because they claim their mortality rate is higher than average.

"Yes, it is an invasion of privacy," says Frederick King, president of the Hooper-Holmes Bureau. But in defense of his business he adds that the person affected "has initiated a request to the insurance company to gamble thousands of dollars on him."[6]

These files are growing. Personal data we don't even know about exist, and even if we knew where to find our dossier, it would be rare that we would get the opportunity to review it.

:

A fully automated system for the measurement of press-relations activity was created in 1964 by PR Data of New York City. Employing a General Electric 225 computer system, the new measurement technique provides the first scientific means for accurately evaluating publicity results. The equipment processes, stores, and reports on each clipped news story that appears in printed media, generating a current and cumulative history of placement in every publication in the nation. Clips from 7,000 daily newspapers, trade journals, business-financial publications and magazines are scanned on a regular basis. The computer is programmed to keep a close record of exposure not only in specific publications, but in specific geographical locations or market centers. Monthly "condition reports" give press relations management the information it needs to maintain a good balance of exposure in each of its distribution locations.

Even leisure-time travel activities are being affected by computerized systems. The day is not far off when it will be difficult to go on a vacation without its being recorded in several files. The largest computer-oriented data processing system to serve the travel and tourist industry was established in July, 1965, by Telemax Corporation. Assisting more than 5,000 subscribers in 145 major cities in North America, it can make reservations and deliver printed confirmations for hotel rooms, motels, rent-a-cars, cruise ships, package tours, and other travel facilities—all within seconds after inquiry.

The Bunker-Ramo Corporation has a telequote time-sharing system in New York City which gives prices on thousands of securities and commodities traded in fifteen different exchanges and more than 1,000 over-the-counter issues, plus other market information. The computer's memory is tapped from compact desk units and the information required is transmitted on a TV-type screen or can be printed out on tape for broker subscriptions.

STATUS, a service of International Telephone and Telegraph Company, can assist organizations by comparing their sales with relevant up-to-date economic indicators found in its data bank.

The business community is rapidly perfecting its computerized personnel systems. It must at all times be willing to take into account reasons for differences between people. Unless data are processed and used with the utmost care, it is possible that what is assumed to be a statistical fact will be really nothing more than a blend of half-truths.

Automated Medicine—The New Doctor Arrives

A stay in the hospital now becomes part of a computer record. MEDLARS is the world's largest medical information storage and retrieval system. At an initial cost of $3 million, it has been operating in Bethesda, Maryland, since July, 1964. The National Library of Medicine began its development of this Medical Literature and Analysis Retrieval System in 1960 in an all-out effort to control the information explosion engulfing medicine.

Each month computers edit and completely cross-reference all unit records stored in it during the previous month. There are more than 12 million coded abstracts of medical records of hospitalized patients already on file; they are accumulated at an average rate of 13,000 per day from more than 360 participating hospitals throughout the United States and Canada. The details on approximately 10 per cent of all hospitalizations in the United States find their way into this data bank. Some doctors predict that computerized medical data banks will provide the needed breakthrough in the conquest of disease and the prolongation of life.

In the last half of 1964, MEDLARS indexed over 16,000 issues of medical journals containing an average of ten articles each. By 1970 MEDLARS will be handling 25,000 issues a year or about 250,000 articles. Its major responsibility is the development of the massive bibliography of the world's medical literature, INDEX MEDICUS.

A computer system in a Kansas City research institute finds new uses for both old and new drugs. The computer is able, within seconds, to correlate the chemical characteristics of any drug with several thousand other drugs. The result is that similarities are suggested, leading to possible new uses.

Electrocardiograms of apparently healthy persons are stored in data banks and compared with profiles of a hundred examples of heart deficiency. When this technique is fully developed, it may be possible to screen the electrocardiograms of entire city populations and identify those who have a tendency toward future heart disorders. The Veterans Administration, at the Bureau of Standards' Washington computer, stores a mass of data on heart disease. Any of ten hospitals hooked up with the computer can relay a patient's electrocardiogram over a telephone wire. In addition to its increased speed and accuracy, Dr. Hubert V. Pipberger reports that it can read far more detail than the human eye can possibly register.

Computers are used to reduce infant mortality and disease. A noted pediatrician, Dr. Sidney Kane, used the storage capacity of a computer to document information related to 150,000 deliveries throughout the country. Records included the mother's age, maternal complications, anesthetics employed and type of delivery. Correlating this data, Dr. Kane hoped to reduce newborn deaths by at least 12,000 to 14,000 annually. Without a computer this research would have required hundreds of man-years of effort.

At Massachusetts General Hospital in Boston, a computer

bank is used to determine all patient medication. As a patient is admitted, a dossier is made on all known illnesses and all drug sensitivities which the patient is known to have as well as the type, amount and frequency of medication needed. All drugs given to the patient are entered and the computer checks to see that dosages do not exceed the safe limits and that no drug is prescribed which might lead to a bad reaction. On the hour, a computer prints out, for every ward in the hospital, a list of the medication due each person, in order of the location of their beds. In addition, the computer drawing on data in storage may send out a report such as "The drug has been administered to this patient for ten consecutive days. Please check with the patient's doctor before further administering of drug."

Recently, two North Carolina hospitals computerized a laboratory where eleven chemical tests are routinely run on the patient's blood, as contrasted with the usual two standard determinations. Unexpected information that was of direct benefit to the patient was found in one out of every fifteen admissions. As anticipated by Paul Armer of the RAND Corporation, the application of computers and information-processing technology to health problems promises significant advances during the next decade.

The computer will take over much of the clerical work and information-handling of those engaged in medical care. This is greatly needed, as studies show that many hospital nurses spend as much as 40 per cent of their time doing clerical work, and that test results and prescription orders may be transcribed as many as ten times.

HIS, Hospital Information System, is a massive installation at Monmouth County Medical Center in Long Branch, New Jersey. The patient's personal data and case history are fed into a computer that initiates service by assigning a bed. The computer proceeds to order appropriate laboratory tests, and informs the kitchen of special dietary requirements. Medication is ordered from the pharmacy, and the computer determines whether the patient is allergic to certain drugs and performs a dosage check.

Hopefully every aspect of patient care is under the watchful electronic memory of HIS. The patient's data are stored in the computer's memory and provide immediate information for care. HIS frees physicians and nurses from workaday tasks and provides them with one of the most precious commodities —time to concentrate on patients. And finally, of course, the computer bills the patient.

The computer technology will also provide more comprehensive information about each individual's medical history. For example, at the Kaiser Hospital in the San Francisco Bay area, every month 4,000 adults receive computerized check-ups. It takes the patient two to three hours to complete a self-administered questionnaire of some 600 items about his medical history; this adds up to an enormous amount of data. Also, tests are recorded for: chest X-ray; mammography for women; electrocardiogram and phonocardiogram, pulse and blood pressure reading; lung capacity test; height, weight and skin-fold thickness (to check for over- and under-weight conditions); hearing and vision.

Application of computers to medical testing will result in cost reductions which, among other effects, will permit significant lowering of the cost of preventive medicine. For example, there are not enough doctors available to administer electrocardiograms to every citizen each year. There is evidence that the computer could at least select those electrocardiograms that require further examination by a cardiologist.

Computers also aid doctors in diagnostic efforts. The computer could suggest tests which would enable the physician to decide among several tentative diagnoses or to confirm the one tentatively arrived at. It is anticipated that in the 1970s the computer should be able to digest facts about the present medical status of individual patients and separate out those cases warranting further attention.

The vital signs of the seriously ill are presently monitored by computers. John A. Osmundsen estimated that as many as ten heart deaths out of a hundred could be prevented if patients were in an intensive coronary care unit where electrocardiograms and pulse rate were continuously monitored.

As a research tool, computers will aid in advancing medical understanding. And finally, computers will assist in the dis-

semination of up-to-date findings and data to doctors throughout the world. A recent World Health Organization review of
computer usage in medicine reported that there was a great
need for an "electronic encyclopedia" of medical knowledge.
This would have an advantage over merely counseling with
other doctors—who may know just as little as the questioning
physician—or turning to a textbook or professional medical
journal, which may be out of date or unavailable.

It has been proven without a doubt that the public benefits,
and that health services have been and will continue to be
improved because of computerized systems. Although there is
a need to caution against release of privy data, for example
telling an employer how sick his worker is, the apparent goals
of medicine are sufficiently satisfying to man that he is willing
to allow as much data as are requested to be assimilated and
processed with the expectation that he will directly benefit.

Playing Games

On the lighter side, during the 1964-65 New York City
World's Fair, an IBM 1440 system was used at the Parker
Pen Pavilion to store the names and particulars of people all
over the world who had indicated an interest in making "pen
pals." Visitors to the pavilion were asked to choose their interests from a list of 389; these were matched, providing a basis
for correspondence with people of similar interests. By the
fair's closing it was expected that over 300,000 names from
all over the world had been matched.

The Monroe Corporation installed two Monrobot XI's in
the business and finance section of the New Jersey Pavilion.
One was used to "measure" visitors' "B. Q." (Behavior Quo-
tient) by matching some basic facts about the visitor with
public norms as established by the Opinion Research Corporation. The other machine printed out information on request
concerning the fifty states.

Another type of data bank that is sweeping the country's
college campuses is computer-based mate-matching services.
One of the more popular ones is "Operation Match" of the
Compatibility Research Corporation in Cambridge, Massachu-

setts, started by several "mixer weary" Harvard juniors. In nine months it collected $300,000 from daters throughout the country. Its advertisement reads: "You may not know it, but you're one in a million. No one else is quite like you—you have different tastes and different attitudes from those of anyone else you know. . . . If you're the modern, adventurous type, you'll probably want to take part in one of the most interesting social experiments ever." A personality test identifies college students and their dating habits; the results are compared with characteristics of over 100,000 other collegians. For $3, your vital statistics are given by mail and placed in an IBM 7090 computer memory file. The computer then scans the qualifications of every member of the opposite sex from your area and selects the five or more matches best for you. Categories covered in the five page inventory are: Absolute Factors, e.g., sex, race, religion, college class, age, height; Identification of Interest, e.g., music, literature, languages, medicine, skiing, television, automobiles; Attitudes Toward, e.g., religion, God, love, marriage, sexual experience; Differing Situations, e.g., opportunity for employment, a completed crossword puzzle, a blind date; Area, e.g., willingness to date out of area; General Information, e.g., smoking habits, drinking habits, academic record, family income, attendance at church or synagogue, College Board Scholastic Aptitude Test verbal and math scores; Semantic Differentials, e.g., how talkative you are, how politically concerned you are, how close your family ties are, how well you like children, how emotional you are; Physical Appearance, e.g., color of your hair and eyes, how you wear your hair, what members of the opposite sex think of you. The idea is not necessarily to match you with someone similar to you, but with someone who meets your specifications.

Where is this information—in which student's closet in the fraternity house, or family attic or unlocked file cabinet? Perhaps it was started just as a spoof, but many thousands of dossiers are on file for students who probably would be shocked if this information were to become public.

Data-Date, an international computer-based dating service, includes a 122-item test. Should it be released for employment or advancement purposes, it would be quite revealing and probably annoying to many. Consider the confidential nature of answers to the following questions:

The trait I am least proud of in myself is—

1) moodiness
2) insecurity
3) timidity
4) coldness
5) instability

At a cocktail party attended by many celebrities, which of the following would most engage your attention and interest—

1) Paul Newman
2) William Buckley
3) Sophia Loren
4) Norman Mailer
5) Nelson Rockefeller
6) Helen Gurley Brown

Of the following, which would you prefer—

1) loving a man who did not love you
2) being loved by a man you could not love
3) neither loving nor being loved until the feeling were mutual, regardless of how long it took to come about

What would you do if your fiancée informs you that she "has had relations with another man"—Would you

1) break the engagement
2) marry her despite grave misgivings
3) tell her it doesn't matter
4) tell her of your own amorous adventures
5) feel that her experience would make for a more successful marriage

Is pre-marital sex—

1) permissible only after engagement
2) permissible only with one you love
3) permissible if the individuals are mature

4) permissible indiscriminately
5) never permissible

The questionnaire is divided into categories. The first emphasizes physical appearance, religion, race, and so on. The second, the psychology of the dater, and the third, individual character traits.

The influence of computerized match-activities has come under attack by the New York City Board of Education, which feels that these services are a "potential danger to physical safety and morals" especially among the teen-age students. They have found that questionnaires circulated around the schoolyards contain such items as:

> True or False: A wide gulf exists today between teen-agers and adults, who are often hostile toward teens. And teens cannot trust what most adults tell them.

> Yes or No: In a broad sense, do your parents know what's happening?

> True or False: I define myself as sexy, in favor of petting, extremely liberal in moral values and of the opinion that the current American attitude toward sex is too conservative.

As Joan and Leslie Rich pointed out in their book *Dating and Mating by Computer,* "there are risks in this sort of enterprise, if unscrupulous elements ever get control of it."[7]

Recently a bookstore salesman in New York's Times Square was charged with violating the state's obscenity laws, and fined $150.[8] He was accused of subscribing to several computer dating services to get names, addresses and telephone numbers of women and then reselling a list of 25 as "available for dates."

His promotional poster read: "Girls Galore—Ages 18–34. Dial a Date. All New York City. Largest List of Names, Addresses and Phones. Just a Phone Call Guarantees a Date." The salesman had organized Tactical Introductions, Inc., selling his list of names at 50 cents a copy to bookstores which resold them for $2.

According to the state's attorney general, the women who participated in the computer matching service but had not agreed to this new bookstore listing suddenly found themselves beset with calls night and day and subjected to "great anxiety and fear."

Automated Education—A New Report Card

In the field of education, data banks are used in a number of services that require information storage and retrieval. The biggest investment in this area is the U.S. government's Education Research Information Center (ERIC). As stated in its announcement, ERIC is a statistical data bank whose basic objective is to provide information on reliable, current, educational research and research-related materials inexpensively to a wide variety of audiences. The value of ERIC will be measured by the degree to which persons anywhere in the country can rely upon the service to inform them of the most important developments in any area of specialization in education. To carry out this goal, ERIC has established eighteen external clearing houses throughout the country, each based on a particular subject-matter area. ERIC acquires, abstracts, indexes, stores, retrieves, and disseminates nationally the most significant and timely educational research and research-related documents.

Project TALENT, administered by the American Institute of Research and supported under grants from the U.S. Office of Education, was the first major effort to establish a data bank in the field of education. It provides a study or inventory of students' abilities and achievements, and contains records of more than 440,000 individuals for a running period of twenty years.

Beginning in 1967 the National Education Association sponsored A Central Computerized Education Staffing Service (ACCESS) for all elementary and secondary teachers and counselors. This is a nation-wide clearing house project to match teachers looking for jobs and superintendents with vacancies to fill.

The program has three basic elements: candidates, who register their qualifications and job preferences by means of a standardized form; employers, who indicate their needs through a standardized vacancy description; and a computer-linkage, an electronic file which seeks to match candidates with appropriate vacancies.

Candidates pay a fee ($8 per year, or until placed if it takes less than a year) to describe their qualifications and preferences, subjects and grade they want to teach, minimum acceptable salary, geographic preference and other choices. The employers pay a minimum search fee of $15 or $4 for each name received. Besides describing the vacancy they seek to fill, they, too, can specify certain preferences as to the candidate's educational attainment or number of years of experience. They can limit the search (and fee) by stipulating the number of names they want referred. The computer then furnishes the names in descending rank order according to how closely they conform to the requirements laid down by the employer. On receiving the results of the search, employers make the next move of getting in touch with the candidates. ACCESS, or NEA-SEARCH as it is often referred to, claims that it is not an evaluator. It is advertised as a locator service, not a placement service; it relies on educational placement officers and others to do the counseling and assessing of candidates. Final decisions remain in the hands of the two parties, who may or may not sign a contract.

The program is based on a computer system specifically prepared for this purpose. One of its unusual features is that it offers candidates the option of "blocking out" their present employers and specifying a preference for a particular type of classroom assignment such as ungraded classes or team teaching.

Through this matching program, the planner hopes to overcome the shortage of teachers and enable more teachers to find the job best suited to their preferences and abilities. As their brochure states, the computer will be used to "provide the dependability and speed of electronic data processing. This efficiency, with the flexibility built into the choices offered employers and teachers, ensures that both can tell the computer what to do for them."

In the initial announcement of the NEA project, there was no mention of confidentiality of information, of who would have access to the data or how the individual applicant would have a controlling power over its future use.

:

Computers and other information technologies will assist in the development of individualized student instruction. One of the present-day failures in education is that the teacher usually prepares lectures with the class group in mind and not with the individual as his central concern. Questions of gearing instruction to the upper, lower or middle levels of capability are still unresolved, which is quite frustrating for teachers and students alike. It is hoped that computers will permit individualized instruction so that each pupil will be able to work at his own pace. One of the leaders in the field of computer-assisted instruction is Patrick Suppes at Stanford University, who is engaged in drill-and-practice in arithmetic. Five levels of difficulty per concept for each grade level in elementary-school mathematics permit the computer to present a level of problem difficulty to the individual student based on his past performance. This is in contrast to the traditional method of giving each student in the class identical problems.

In New York's P.S. 175 in Harlem, a computer and tape recorder are hooked up to a talking typewriter. A child listens to a voice saying the letter "c" and is asked to watch the red pointer as it moves to "c." The student is instructed now to find "c" on the keyboard and press it. The voice repeats itself every few seconds until the child finds the right key. Four-year-olds using this computer-assisted form of instruction have been able to write entire sentences in just four months. Six-year-olds have edited their own newspaper with stories, rhymes and riddles.

Hopefully, with the aid of computers, students will be assigned courses that meet their needs. West of Chicago, at the Riverside-Brookfield High School, profiles of students including scores from standard test batteries and classroom achievement are fed into computers. The school staff expects that this data could be used to determine whether the student should take a French or calculus course, and even to project his probable grade.

The computer may also be a powerful tool in educational

research and development since more complex information and greater volumes of data can be handled. With human behavior programmed by computer, we may uncover yet more about man's learning processes.

Doubtless, computers will play an increasing role in attempting to improve and upgrade education over the next few decades. Already at work on clerical aspects of education, computers will continue to help reduce the paperwork and the analysis of data. The "ideal" utilization of a teacher's time could be determined, and the reduction of administrative activities would release him for teaching. In California a pilot study revealed that computerized grade-reporting added at least four effective teaching-days to the academic school year.

Within the next decade we can also anticipate that the computer will be used by teachers for processing information. Terminals, specialized typewriters connected to the computer, will be distributed throughout school systems, ready and waiting for instructions from the teacher to answer questions. Certainly the student, teacher and administrator will have found a new friend in the computer. But they will discover that through this friendship they are able to learn just about everything there is to know about each other as a result of the growth of information files. Don D. Bushnell, a leader in the field of computerized educational technology and assistant director of the Brooks Foundation, Santa Barbara, California, identifies major issues that must be resolved. Should the data file be open to the public or will it be appropriately screened so that only educational management has access to all the data? What information is appropriate for the teachers, the guidance personnel, and the student, are as yet unanswered questions.

A Behavioral Research Data Bank

Why we do or do not buy a particular brand of food or clothing may no longer be part of our private world. One of the most remarkable applications of the data bank concept can be found in the field of marketing research, especially as it relates to consumer motivation. Some of the questions that marketers want answered are: What is the motivation of the buyer? What causes him to buy one product instead of another? What terms can be used to describe the emotional or psychological milieu surrounding the consumer? The solution to these and other motivational problems will come from research which will require an enormous number of personal details and behavior records.

In one effort to establish a behavioral data bank, RCA donated its Model 301 computer to the Roper Public Opinion Research Center at Williams College in Massachusetts. Linked by telephone to the University of California at Berkeley, to M.I.T. and to the University of Michigan, it is used to memorize the answers to some 400 million questions asked in public opinion polls since 1936.

Recently there has been a growing movement within the social sciences to establish an information repository or data bank. Its major function would be locating relevant data and ancillary information about society and arranging for their acquisition, reproduction and subsequent circulation to the community. This effort has been called the Council of Social Science Data Archives. By interaction with other data-collecting organizations, theories in the social sciences can be more adequately researched and tested. For example, it will be possible to determine more accurately the relationship between individuals and their environment; individuals' characteristics can be studied more precisely if their behavior is tied in with information about their income, community, choice of employment, and so on. The Council's counterparts in Europe are UNESCO in Paris and the International Social Science Council.

The system as proposed will make it possible to enlarge the scope of statistical and social analysis. An increasing number of variables could be included in the evaluation, i.e., geography, labor-force characteristics, and political statistics. In addition, the Council of Social Science Data Archives (coordinated at the Bureau of Applied Research at Columbia University) should make it easier to create better research designs for future experimentation and inquiry; to control and improve historical analysis; to identify areas for upgrading education; and to be of considerable assistance in determining a wide variety of policies. The increase in data accumulation would be of assistance studying the lives of the poor, minority groups and city residents. It would assist governmental agencies at all levels in their anti-poverty programs.

As suggested in an article by Ralph Bisco of the Inter-University Consortium for Political Research: "It is convenient to have two classifications of archives: 1) general purpose service archives, those whose data are routinely available to the academic community as a whole, and 2) local service archives, those which acquire data and provide services only for a geographically limited group of users."[9] At the time of writing, nineteen data agencies had agreed to participate.

The Roper Public Opinion Research Center in Williamstown, mentioned above, is the oldest, largest general-purpose social science archive of computer-readable information in the United States, and probably in the world. The center has in storage the equivalent of more than eight million IBM cards of information: raw data from over four thousand studies from 22 American suppliers and 71 other organizations located in 41 countries abroad. The Roper organization maintains survey records about politics, use of mass media, consumer buying and related topics.

In collaboration with the Institute for International Studies, the International Data Library and Reference Service was established in 1958 at the University of California. In recent years it has become a general-purpose service archive emphasizing a rapidly growing subset of its total holdings, i.e., sample survey and poll data from developing countries, particularly in Latin America and Asia. Presently the archive maintains over a hundred different studies from about ten African countries, fifteen from Latin countries and about twenty from Japan. Information has also been acquired from India, the Phillipines, Malaysia, Pakistan, Turkey and Thailand. Over seventy studies have been processed for more universal and powerful analyses.

Organized in 1962, the Inter-University Consortium for Political Research is a partnership between the University of Michigan's Survey Research Center of the Institute for Social Research and about sixty universities and nonprofit research organizations in the United States, Canada, Great Britain and

Europe. An early effort led to the acquisition of all of the major political surveys of the past twenty-five years. Studies were also conducted on all persons who have served in the United States Congress; election statistics for political units below the county unit; selected state referenda votes by county; and legislative roll calls.

The Louis Harris Political Data Center, established in 1965, is a repository for information accumulated by Lou Harris during his years of survey and polling work. It contains sample surveys of various regions of the United States. A considerable amount of the data relate to Southern politics.

The U.S. Bureau of Labor Statistics and the U.S. Bureau of the Census also are participating. The Labor Statistics group is reporting information each month on the National Industry Statistics, on State and Area Industry Statistics and Labor Force Statistics. The data from these three programs are prepared for processing by the Manpower Information System. The Bureau of the Census, because of its concern about the confidentiality of data, only permits a small portion of its information to be made available to the social science community.

The Center for International Studies at M.I.T. has recoded and reprocessed a considerable amount of data from the Roper Center for use in their analyses. The M.I.T. Center maintains information about the political and social behavior of entire populations or particular sub-groups in Europe, Asia and Latin America.

The University of Iowa operates a Laboratory for Political Research. It contains sample surveys, legislative roll calls and statistics about the politics of Iowa secured by commercial polling agencies, scholars and the government.

In 1964 a data repository was organized within the Survey Research Laboratory of the University of Illinois. It contains surveys and statistics secured by scholars and government agencies about the economic, social and political characteristics of Illinois.

The U.C.L.A. Political Behavior Archive, founded in 1961, is a data bank including official government statistics, election returns, survey data and biographical materials. Much of its biographical and survey data is on political recruitment and career patterns from many countries.

A number of foreign data archives include: DATUM (Documentation and Training Center for Theory and Methods of Regional Research) in West Germany, the Social and Economic Archive Committee in England, and agencies at the University of Cologne and the University of Amsterdam.

When Donald Michael of the Center for Research on the Utilization of Scientific Knowledge said, "The overriding questions of course will be *who* is to decide *whom* is to be manipulated and for *what* ends,"[11] he was referring to Bill S.836 to create a National Social Science Foundation and a "Full Opportunity and Social Accounting Act."

Lou Harris, who is leading the crusade in support of the foundation, said, "Frankly, I think many of the critics of the collection of data are not familiar with the modern techniques of computer analysis, the researcher could not care less about the private affairs of the individual."[12] But many of the critics are familiar with computer technology. One of the outspoken critics of the Social Accounting Act is Herbert Gans of the Center for Urban Education and professor of sociology and education at Columbia, who warns:

> The prime function of social-economic accounting is to gather data on the benefits and costs of various governmental programs, and on the effectiveness with which these programs reach their intended clients. Consequently, social-economic accounting will probably invade the privacy of government agencies to carry out programs without knowing their effectiveness more than it will invade the privacy of individuals. . . . Even so, there is a possibility that socio-economic accounting studies will require data from individuals about their activities and opinions which could be used to injure them.[13]

Recently the Behavioral Sciences Division of the National Academy of Sciences established a permanent committee on information to explore the advantages of having a data repository. In early 1968 a report, "Communication Systems and Resources in the Behavioral Sciences," was submitted; it urged the development of a computerized information system to keep the flow of research data below "flood heights."

In his support of a behavioral science center, Kingsley Davis, chairman of the Division of Behavioral Sciences at the Council of Social Science Data Archives, put a word of caution: "To many social scientists the potential developments sketched in the report may seem like '1984' but there can be no doubt that somehow the horse-and-buggy methods of social researchers will have to give way to new methods made possible by modern communications technology."[10] An obvious sanction, but with a note of concern.

The Legal Profession Gets Computerized

In 1964 state and federal officials were extremely impressed when John Horty, head of the Health Law Center at the University of Pittsburgh, demonstrated the first operational system for automated statute research. The officials simply posed questions to the computer in everyday language and received print-outs on any phase of existing local laws including, where desired, complete text of all statutes and sections relevant to any given issue.

Horty and his staff have been working since 1959 to devise a computer system for storing laws and for obtaining responses to many types of legal questions. In 1960 Horty created a mild sensation in a notoriously conservative profession by showing the American Bar Association what his "automatic law clerk" could do with answers to questions concerning tax exemptions in the fifty states and the District of Columbia. In less than ten minutes it analyzed 400 statutes and typed out all citations.

The laws are put on tape in their entirety. To obtain information, the lawyer speaks into the computer words he selects as pertinent to his topic; then the machine furnishes the citations to all laws containing these words, and provides the full text if desired. For most of the questions, the process takes only a small fraction of the time it would take a lawyer or clerk to do the same job. For example, in a recent demonstration the computer reviewed up to 30,000 statutes and produced the desired citations in less than twenty minutes. For some legal work, all words of all statutes must be scanned. In the Pittsburgh program, an inverted file scheme permits a first run-down to see in which statutes or sections a word is to be found, before the statute itself is retrieved.

Law cases can be stored together with relevant information. Within a twenty-four-hour period the lawyer is provided with a complete dossier on prior cases and decisions. In the past this information for determining precedent often took a week or more to find. Now 6,230,000 words of Pennsylvania law are placed on four reels of tape in the Pittsburgh program. Major words referring to a specific type of action are fed to the machine, and following a search of less than a minute, the pertinent case citations are produced. Once the status of the case is determined, summaries of past cases similar to the one under consideration are obtained to provide precedents. Summaries include names, dates, decisions, appeals and counter-appeals. Data are produced to determine the acceptability of witnesses. Computer print-outs have been used to decide whether it would be better to appear before a judge or have the matter go to a jury.

In 1967 the Belgian government created a center for research and documentation—Credoc. Eventually, all Belgian law will be placed in a computer's memory; the project will commence with 150,000 documents in civil law. According to Monsieur E. Houtart, a Brussels lawyer and one of the four directors of Credoc, ". . . it would not only save time and energy for lawyers, but also result in a far more efficient legal system." For to handle the sale of the apartment of a minor by his legal guardian, a lawyer might spend days finding the appropriate law. With the new system, the lawyer could simply call the Credoc center and ask for references. He would get chapter and verse of statutes, previous judgments and applicable learned studies. The service also will have relevance for judges—especially those judges who often deliver opinions without full knowledge of legal precedents because they do not have the time to look up the law in the only complete law library in the country, the bar library of Brussels.

The United States Air Force contracted to enable military administrators to find U.S. Code provisions and decisions of the U.S. Comptroller General relevant to fiscal law. Under Project LITE (Legal Information Through Electronics), the service has stored the full text of the U.S. Code, all published decisions of the Comptroller General, the armed services procurement regulations and other regulatory material. These represent 40 million words of text; on tape an incredibly fast search can be made of all this material.

A Univac III, programmed by Law Research Services, Inc., established a library of more than a million case references in December, 1963. A comprehensive indexing program permits the computer to test the relevance of the cases to many legal research problems at the rate of 120,000 cases per minute. Relevant cases are checked for prior history, and their current status is determined in a predating and updating process. Computer results are then reviewed with outside authorities and checked for relevance and authenticity by Law Research Services staff. More than 4,000 attorneys are currently subscribers to the system (at a fee of $25 per inquiry) and the New York bar associations are cooperating in helping defray the cost of the service to younger lawyers.

The superior court in Los Angeles County is the largest judiciary system that has turned to computers. In 1964, 21,000 cases were awaiting assignment to trial, which is usually scheduled two years in the future; now the backlog is down to 9,000 cases, of which 6,000 have been assigned trial dates within six months. The computer is loaded with precise information—which courtrooms are available, how long a case is expected to last, which of the 8,000 attorneys practicing before the superior court will try a specific case and how heavy the load of the courts will be. The Los Angeles computer's other chief target at present is traffic offenses. The municipal court houses a central traffic index which will have terminals in more than twenty municipal courtrooms in the county. When an offender appears to plead his case, the computer immediately determines whether he has other tickets outstanding. It also tracks down motorists who have been ignoring traffic tickets.

Information retrieval from data banks is used to detect and prevent crime. In Los Angeles, the sheriff's office has in storage a computer system containing all records and *modus operandi* of 2½ million known offenders. The system stores data on the more than 2 million cars registered in the county; the approximately 44,000 stolen cars reported in the county; the average of 10,000 persons in jail at a given time; and the 1,000 who have served their sentences and enter the outside world each day. The computer system proponents expect that the crime rate will be reduced and that time, effort and human life will be saved. Upon apprehension of a suspect, the officer on duty radios headquarters, and within moments the computer network retrieves the desired data from its memory and sends it back to the police officer.

One computerized crime data center is in trouble. After several years of study, the New York State Identification and Intelligence System (N.Y.S.I.I.S.) was ready in the beginning of 1968 to become operational. The system has 503 employees and an annual budget of $5.2 million. It was created to develop an automated information-sharing system to service 3,600 police and sheriff departments, district attorneys, courts and correctional agencies. It was also designed to include intelligence on crime, an automated fingerprint identification system, a criminal history file and a list of stolen property.

Now it appears that some law-enforcement agencies are reluctant to release or share their information on organized crime. A spokesman for the state said: "When it gets right down to it, I just don't know whether Hogan [New York County District Attorney] is going to let N.Y.S.I.I.S. see the sensitive kind of stuff he's got in his files, especially when there's a possibility it might fall into the hands of a corrupt sheriff or police chief at the other end of the state."[14] Fifteen million dollars has been spent and now the state officials may find that there are not enough participants to warrant a complete go-ahead. Obviously even within the system itself, the civil servant, for one reason or another, may be hesitant to release data he and his staff have worked so hard and long to collect.

A $4.7 million contract to IBM was awarded by New York City, the first city in the country to build a computerized police dispatch system. Known as SPRINT for Special Police

Radio Inquiry Network, it is expected to be operational around 1970. A call for police assistance would be handled this way:

> The officer receiving the call presses keys on his terminal to identify the borough, location and type of incident. After checking a display of this data on his screen, he transmits it to the computer by touching another key.
>
> The computer checks the data and informs the officer of errors, such as a non-existent address, by flashing a message on the terminal screen. It then searches an electronic location file and determines the block number, precinct, nearest intersection and nearest hospital.
>
> This information, along with the numbers of three available patrol cars, is flashed to the appropriate one of several additional terminals manned by radio dispatchers, each of whom covers a specific area of the city. The dispatcher then orders a car to the scene, informing the computer of his action through his keyboard.[15]

One of the giant efforts in police circles is PIN, standing for Police Information Network. It is used in a nine-county area around San Francisco Bay to integrate information through a centralized electronic file of warrants of arrest. With PIN, for example, a police officer who stops a motorist can radio ahead to his headquarters the license-plate number and name; then the information is typed into an inquiry terminal connected over a communications network to a computer. Within two minutes the policeman knows whether any warrants are outstanding against the person in any of the ninety-three law-enforcement districts and whether the car is stolen or wanted in connection with another crime.

:

The data bank of Alexandria, Virginia, is organized around property; it contains data about the city organized into two master files of use to property lawyers. The street section file contains 120 items of data about the 3,518 blocks and intersections of Alexandria; the parcel file contains 91 types of data about 20,000 parcels of land. Within one week, six governmental managers made requests for information similar to the following:

> Survey all intersections in the city showing those where five or more accidents occurred in the past three months and give the characteristics of each such intersection.

> For two proposed urban renewal areas, analyze the density and location of welfare cases, minimum housing-code violations, health hazards, fires, mortalities, crimes, and arrests.

All six of the requests were completed and drawn from the data bank within the same week at a total computer rental cost of $67.50 and three hours of staff time.

According to IBM systems planner (and lawyer) Norbert A. Halloran, every urban area may be able to have its own full-scale "judicial data center." He suggests that a data center, updated daily, could provide a continuous flow of information to lawyers and judges, enabling them to work far more efficiently than is possible today.

Citizens' reactions to these innovations are sometimes surprising. When New York City started using a computer to cope with its traffic-court problems, news reports warned that the machine would be able to track down scofflaws in 45 days rather than 18 months. The city's receipts of fines from traffic violators rose tenfold.

Even some of the larger law firms, e.g., Cravath, Swaine and Moore, are finding computers valuable. Property records usually are filed in large, prebound folios, written in longhand and stored in county courthouses. Searching property records is considered by many the most dreary of all routine legal tasks. To overcome this burden, King County in Seattle, Washington, installed an IBM 360 to keep property records and prepare tax statements. Before this innovation it took a double shift of eighteen people about nine weeks to compute and mail out some 500,000 tax statements; now it is done in a week. Records are stored magnetically in a small central data file rather than in several large rooms. From the 2,000 magnetic strips holding up to 800 million pieces of information,

it takes only seconds to retrieve property or tax records showing the taxpayer's name, property description, valuation and
improvements. Property owners, mortgage companies, lawyers,
title companies, and county officials, to name just a few, have
access to the system, while the county courthouse has several
keyboard terminals to query the computer. The computer
system supplies a printed abstract or displays it on small
television screens. County officials claim this system makes it
easier to find delinquent taxpayers, to make accurate appraisals, to determine allocation of tax receipts and to study
usage of land and buildings.

Some serious students of the legal profession are concerned
about many of these innovations. There is a growing reaction
to the possibility that computers may provide a way to predict the outcome of decisions—even those of the United States
Supreme Court, thereby defeating the purpose of judging.
And there are others who challenge the accumulation of too
much data about too many people.

A judicial computer set up in a county-wide electronic
data-processing system could provide instant information on
a particular case directly to the litigating lawyer in his office,
as well as to the trial judge. With special typewriters linked
to this data center, a lawyer could retrieve information on past
trial court cases—available today in only a few courts. Court
orders, summonses, and judgment notices could be prepared
automatically and sent directly to the lawyer's office. Some
are at work devising methods for screening out jurors. It is
technically possible to give prospective jurors tests and analyze the results by computer to determine the composition of
a jury.

Computers are also bringing greater strength to rulings by
Washington's regulatory agencies. The Federal Trade Commission, the Interstate Commerce Commission, the Justice
Department's Antitrust Division and others are looking at ways
to adapt to computers. Traditionally, they have the authority
to determine what data are relevant to proceedings and to
decide how information should be correlated and analyzed.
Commissioners make decisions on findings growing out of
these data. Unless an agency's judgment is arbitrary or clearly
irrational, courts will sustain its findings under the doctrine

of "primary jurisdiction" developed by the Supreme Court over the past 60 years.

At present, even if an agency's reasoning in a case is obscure, a regulated industry or some other litigant usually has a tough job winning reversal of a ruling in court. The judge presumes the agency decision is correct, and the private plaintiff must shoulder the burden of proof. Now the computer, with its ability to spin out mathematical correlations and refine data, may make the litigant's job even tougher. At the very least, he will have to contend with mounting piles of evidence supporting the agency's stand and enhanced with a "prepared by computer" imprint.

However, Roy N. Freed, counsel for Honeywell's Computer Control Division, expects the same government-operated computers to let litigants see for the first time into the darkness surrounding agency regulations: "If agencies adopt computers they will have to make their formulas more precise and hence courts will be more informed."[16] In order to adapt computers to such regulatory procedures as rate-making, specific and detailed programs must be written. A private litigant could introduce the program as evidence in court, and if an agency's rulings were bitterly contested, according to Freed, "the agency would have to prove its mathematical models valid. It would have to put economists and programmers on the stand." Rather than relying on vague expertise of the agency, Freed believes, the court would look at the assumptions behind the program to determine whether a ruling was rational. In other words, the litigant could force the agency to present a stronger justification of its results.

In the United States today, the issue of "law and order" is dominant. As programs are developed to prevent crime and violence; as new technology is brought to bear on lawlessness; as information clearing houses are designed to wage war on civic disorder, it is essential that our nation's leaders be sufficiently enlightened not to sacrifice individual privacy to the goal of fighting crime.

:

The data banks and computer installations described are but a sample of the many now in existence. The present num-

ber of such systems is dwarfed when compared to the quantity
of data banks projected for the future.

As early as 1965 Thomas C. Rowan, vice-president of the
System Development Corporation, stated: "As expanding applications of information make it possible to combine record
systems . . . to have, in short, an individual's entire history,
private as well as public, stored on a small bit of magnetic
tape and perhaps too easily accessible for too many purposes,
the issue of privacy becomes increasingly important."[17]

M. R. Maron of the RAND Corporation added his opinion
of the way machines make decisions about people: "How does
an individual get an opportunity to 'tell the system' that its
selective criteria don't apply to his own special case? . . . Each
individual is different, each has certain extenuating circumstances, each has information which he believes to be relevant
to the selection decision and which the system does not consider relevant. If an individual does not have the opportunity
to be judged on the circumstances of his own special situation,
then he is being treated as a machine."[18]

There is little doubt that as computerized systems spread
throughout the nation and world, surveillance by data processing is bound to increase. If the trend continues, it will soon
be possible to have all personal information about an individual gathered on a continuous basis and held indefinitely until
requested. The snowballing effect is quite pronounced here.
When the decision is made to purchase a computer, more
data are gathered about the employees, customers or taxpayers
who are of interest to an organization. Although this may
provide for better services, improved decision-making and
policy-programming, it also provides personal information
about individuals never known before the advent of computers.

One of the giants in developing advanced computers, Professor Robert Fano, Director of Project MAC's time-sharing
computer system at M.I.T., was quite aware that his work
could enhance the computer's ability to collect and store more
and more information about people:

> The very power of advanced computer systems makes
> them a serious threat to privacy of the individual. If
> every significant action is recorded in the mass memory

of a community computer system, and programs are available for analyzing them, the daily activities of each individual could become open to scrutiny.

While the technical means may be available for preventing illegal searches, where will society draw the line between legal and illegal? Will the custodians of the system be able to resist pressure from government agencies, special interest groups, and powerful individuals? And what about the custodians themselves? Can society trust them with so much power? . . . The danger lies in ourselves. Through mental laziness, or fear of accepting responsibility, or just plain neglect we may delegate to computers prerogatives that should remain ours.[19]

The dangers of data leakage by nongovernmental organizations may in the future be even greater than within the government. Computerized systems, many of the time-sharing type, are not within federal control and therefore the legal boundaries concerning them are ill defined. Consequently, the citizen or employee not only does not know how data about him is collected, stored and revealed, but has not been told how this information is made secure. Either deliberately or by accident, computerized files could easily be passed from person to person. In addition, since many of our large organizations are spread throughout the country, data will conceivably be moved about from one location to another, opening opportunities for tapping and for altering files.

The day must come when the government will impose standards, backed by law, demanding that their nonfederal counterparts adopt safeguards. To require a detailed "protection" analysis might force organizations to comply with safeguards, encourage them to re-examine what they are doing and possibly even eliminate the data-bank concept. To assist these organizations, the computer manufacturers should provide a detailed statement to each purchaser-user, clearly identifying the technological safeguards that have been placed within the installation.

Failure to do this will produce the inevitable threat of data surveillance that will leave the citizen unprotected from examination; his actions will be dictated by a fear of total exposure.

CHAPTER IV

A Study of
the Computerized
Business Community

There is even less protection against mismanagement of data within the computer systems in business than within government. Federal restrictions in governmental agencies may not apply in guarding against possible corporate misuse of employees' personal information. Not only is the worker ignorant of what personal data are collected and distributed; he has even less knowledge as to how it may be kept. By error or design, an employee's files may be freely exchanged.

The need of business for information of all kinds is accepted largely without question. In spring 1968 a graduate seminar at Columbia University, chaired by the author,* attempted to determine the effect computerization—contrasted with manual file systems—has on the collection of personnel records. A random sample of 1,000 was drawn from a list of the leading 15,000 U.S. corporations, each employing anywhere from

* Students were David Brandenburg, Vera Calvo, Lynn Harvey, Cecil Jones, Anton Mallner, Gary McLean, Norman Reimer, Alan Schwartz, John Sullivan and Herbert Wollowick.

5 to 200,006 workers. The analysis was based on a 13.3 per cent return of a detailed questionnaire.

Access

How does computerization affect personnel data systems? Computerized systems provide greater *access* to employee information for the worker himself, his supervisor and government agencies—but not for other business organizations. One possible explanation for this is that the companies that use computers have more enlightened personnel policies than those that do not.

Computerized systems increase feedback to the employee of what information is kept on him. This may be accomplished through regular counseling sessions with his supervisors. It may also be that computers facilitate the feedback to the employee because it is easier to show the employee a printout from the computer than his entire personnel jacket, which might contain information that he is not permitted to see. Extracting specific information is difficult with a manual system. By the same token, companies find it easier to provide the government with information from computers.

It is significant that other businesses have no greater access to company records that have been computerized, for this might constitute the greatest threat to individual privacy in the area of employment opportunities.

For the reader who wishes a more thorough analysis of the study, the statistical tables on pages 76–79 indicate exactly who has access to personnel items contained in computers and manual files.

Effects of Computerization

This study shows that some companies have still not discovered all the capabilities of a computer in a personnel department. The findings indicate that much of the information already collected dealt more with accounting than personnel matters. In time, companies may well expand the uses of computers in personnel departments.

It was assumed that, as time passed, companies would *store* increasing amounts of data in computerized systems because they would realize that these highly efficient systems were underutilized and be tempted to use them more and more. However, this is not the case for personnel records.

The companies studied utilized computers primarily for accounting purposes. This might be explained by the fact that using computers for accounting and payroll saves money over the long run, but that in most instances it would probably not be worth the cost to use computers just to organize personnel data. It is also probable that the companies that do use computers for more than accounting, do so only after making a careful study of which personal data are essential and which are useless. This process results in the discarding of much data. Therefore the mere fact that time passes does not mean that more personal data are added to the computer.

The findings also show that since the cost factor is central in management's decision as to what to put on their computers, computer-owning companies with sizeable files of information find it economical to put more of that information on their system, while companies that own a computer but have relatively little data on their employees do not find it economical to put additional personnel data on their computer.

Relation to Company Size

It is widely believed that computers are used more by large companies than by smaller ones; and that it is the large companies who have accumulated more total personnel information, both manually and on computer. This study suggests that neither of these statements is accurate. There is a possible explanation of why large companies may not necessarily collect more information on each employee. In smaller companies it may be easier to collect many types of information. As an example, in this study the company that employed five people collected all 41 possible pieces of information, while the company employing 200,006 people collected only 17 items out of 41. There may also be greater need for information when people work closely with each other, as in a very small company.

Actually, the decision on how much data to collect seems not to relate to company size; it is more a question of the

Item	Employee		Immediate Supervisor		Government		Non-Government (Other Companies)	
	Yes	No	Yes	No	Yes	No	Yes	No
1. Current income	32	22	46	8	31	23	2	52
2. Past income	17	13	24	6	15	15	2	28
3. Outstanding debts	1	1	1	1	1	1	0	2
4. Insurance carried (addition to company)	4	3	5	2	2	5	0	7
5. Outside employment	1	2	2	1	0	3	0	3
6. Monthly living expenses	—	—	—	—	—	—	—	—
7. House—owned or rented	—	—	—	—	—	—	1	1
8. Automobile—type and year	1	0	0	1	0	1	0	2
9. Test scores (employment and promotional)	0	2	1	1	0	2	0	2
10. References	—	—	—	—	—	—	—	—
11. Dismissals	1	4	4	1	2	3	0	5
12. Job title	11	11	18	4	7	15	2	20
13. Suggestions submitted by employee	1	0	1	0	0	1	0	1
14. Transfer requests	—	—	—	—	—	—	—	—
15. Merit ratings	4	3	5	2	1	6	0	7
16. Awards, achievements, etc.	1	2	1	2	1	2	0	3
17. Job potential	1	2	2	1	0	3	0	3
18. Skills inventory	1	3	3	1	0	4	0	4
19. Absenteeism	11	7	15	3	3	15	1	17
20. Institutions attended	5	4	8	1	3	6	0	9

21. Class standing	3	0	3	0	1	2	0	3
22. Major field	4	3	7	1	1	7	1	7
23. Extra-curricular activities	3	3	4	2	1	4	0	6
24. Degrees obtained	4	4	6	2	1	7	0	8
25. Past residences	2	1	3	0	1	2	0	3
26. Race	1	5	3	3	1	5	0	6
27. Religious beliefs	—	—	—	—	—	—	—	—
28. Domestic harmony	—	—	—	—	—	—	—	—
29. Relatives employed by company	—	—	—	—	—	—	—	—
30. Occupations of others in family	—	—	—	—	—	—	—	—
31. Health of relatives and family	—	—	—	—	—	—	—	—
32. Military status	3	6	7	2	0	9	0	9
33. Military experience	3	1	3	1	0	4	1	3
34. Criminal record	2	1	1	2	0	3	1	2
35. Hobbies	2	0	1	1	0	2	0	2
36. Community involvement	0	2	1	1	0	2	0	2
37. Political affiliations	—	—	—	—	—	—	—	—
38. Physical health	1	0	1	0	0	1	0	1
39. Emotional stability	—	—	—	—	—	—	—	—
40. Results of personal investigations	—	—	—	—	—	—	—	—
41. History of alcoholism, drug addiction, etc.	—	—	—	—	—	—	—	—

ACCESS TO MANUAL RECORDS* ON EMPLOYEES

Item	Employee		Immediate Supervisor		Government		Non-Government (Other Companies)	
	Yes	No	Yes	No	Yes	No	Yes	No
1. Current income	31	32	49	14	29	34	8	55
2. Past income	41	42	56	27	36	47	3	78
3. Outstanding debts	9	18	11	16	5	22	1	26
4. Insurance carried (addition to company)	5	12	7	10	2	15	0	17
5. Outside employment	9	19	17	11	6	22	0	28
6. Monthly living expenses	3	6	4	5	2	7	0	9
7. House—owned or rented	21	28	31	18	10	39	1	48
8. Automobile—type and year	13	19	17	15	8	24	1	31
9. Test scores (employment and promotional)	25	59	61	23	16	68	1	83
10. References	20	97	80	37	21	96	3	114
11. Dismissals	25	74	67	32	22	77	5	93
12. Job title	42	54	73	23	30	66	15	80
13. Suggestions submitted by employee	24	31	37	18	7	48	3	52
14. Transfer requests	29	51	48	32	11	69	3	77
15. Merit ratings	82	48	61	19	17	63	2	78
16. Awards, achievements, etc.	27	33	41	21	12	50	3	59
17. Job potential	11	38	40	9	9	40	3	46
18. Skills inventory	18	38	43	13	7	49	2	54
19. Absenteeism	32	67	83	16	25	74	11	88
20. Institutions attended	49	63	88	24	35	87	8	104

21. Class standing	23	38	42	19	10	51	3	58
22. Major field	42	50	73	18	18	73	5	85
23. Extra-curricular activities	31	42	58	15	15	59	4	69
24. Degrees obtained	45	60	85	20	21	84	8	97
25. Past residences	32	47	50	29	20	59	6	72
26. Race	8	14	14	8	8	13	1	20
27. Religious beliefs	1	9	6	4	2	8	0	10
28. Domestic harmony	4	9	9	4	2	11	2	11
29. Relatives employed by company	32	56	60	28	22	66	6	82
30. Occupations of others in family	12	22	24	10	7	27	1	33
31. Health of relatives and family	7	16	9	14	4	19	0	23
32. Military status	46	59	73	32	24	81	8	97
33. Military experience	40	53	68	25	21	72	8	85
34. Criminal record	25	52	48	29	14	63	3	74
35. Hobbies	22	40	40	21	12	50	5	56
36. Community involvement	19	25	29	15	11	33	4	38
37. Political affiliations	3	6	7	2	3	6	0	9
38. Physical health	36	64	66	34	17	83	4	96
39. Emotional stability	4	20	12	12	3	21	1	23
40. Results of personal investigations	12	68	51	27	12	66	1	77
41. History of alcoholism, drug addiction, etc.	7	36	23	20	7	36	1	34

* *Manual* includes: files, keysort systems, keypunch systems, and microfilms.

personnel director's preference. For instance, he might prefer to use manual files because they are usually stored in his office, and come under his total control.

Summary

The following points emerge: a company's size has no relation to the use of a computer and to the amount of information collected; the length of time with a computer does not increase the amount of information collected; computers increase the access of certain groups to personal information; and the more data a computer-owning company has, the more it puts on the computer.

We see from this study that companies often do not make full use of their computers for storing personal data. But it is also true that the more data companies do collect, the more are likely to be put on a computerized system. This factor, combined with the greater accessibility of the computer, may lead to increasing misuse of personal information; therefore it seems clear that in the future greater controls of access will have to be established.

CHAPTER V

Babbage's Dream Come True—
The Technical Feasibility

A computerized system containing data for every man, woman and child in the United States—received from any form or questionnaire they have ever filled out—is within current capability. All these facts could be gathered in one building and could be transmitted along a telephone line within a few minutes. And there are experts who anticipate computers that will be 10,000 times as powerful as today's computers. David Sarnoff, the guiding spirit of the Radio Corporation of America, claimed that by 1976 a computer will be capable of making 400 trillion computations an hour—or two billion computations an hour for every man, woman and child.[1]

Dr. Richard W. Hamming, director of mathematical research at Bell Telephone Laboratories, noted that most major industrial revolutions were initiated by changes on the order of magnitude of 10. For example, the first steam engine was about 10 times as effective as animal power. Steam locomotives and automobiles were about 10 times faster than animal-drawn carriages, as was the case of the airplane's speed compared with the speed of the car. Computers, however, according to Hamming, are about 60 to 70 times more powerful than their predecessors. In addition, they are up to 10 million times faster than the mechanical calculators that they are replacing.[2]

Victor Hugo once said that there was nothing more powerful than an idea whose time has arrived. This was certainly true of the computer. However, it was to be a long while before its modern application took the form of the wondrous systems of today.

Blaise Pascal, born on June 19, 1623, in Central France, is probably the first great name associated with the mechanization of the calculator. His many contributions in thirty-nine short years of life are today still amazing. By the age of twelve he was already familiar with the purposes of mathematics, and by sixteen he had written a paper that was acclaimed as the beginning of modern projective geometry. While still in his teens, Blaise Pascal invented, built and sold the first operating calculating machine. For three years nothing else mattered to him but how well his calculator was coming along. Assisted by some mechanics, he made over fifty models, some of wood, others of ebony and copper. By the time of his twenty-second birthday he had completed his "pascaline."[3]

Unlike Pascal, Gottfried Wilhelm Leibniz, born on June 21, 1646, in Leipzig, Germany, was favored with a long life and chose to pursue most of the intellectual activities of the day. He studied various designs and set himself the task of constructing a more perfect and efficient machine. First he improved Pascal's device by adding a stepped-cylinder to represent the digits one through nine. Leibniz was also determined to have a machine that would not merely add and subtract, but would also multiply, divide and extract square roots without error. He strongly felt: "It is unworthy of excellent men to lose hours like slaves in the labor of calculation which could safely be relegated to anyone else if machines were used."[4] In 1694 he built a calculating machine that was indeed far superior to Pascal's and presented the first general-purpose calculating device to answer the major needs of mathematicians.

The unsung hero of the computer was Charles Babbage,

born on December 26, 1792, in Totnes, Devonshire, England. During his stay at Cambridge University, his studies led him into a critical examination of the logarithmic tables used in making accurate calculations. The time and labor required to construct these tables were great. During one of his freer moments, Babbage was contemplating this problem while sitting in a room of the Analytical Society. One of his friends came in, and seeing him off in a far world, asked: "Well, Babbage, what are you dreaming about?" Pointing to some tables of logarithms, Babbage replied: "I am thinking that all these tables might be calculated by machinery."[5] He was forever calling to the attention of scientific societies the number and importance of errors in astronomical tables and calculation.

For the remainder of his life, he pursued this interest. He was convinced that it was technically feasible to construct a machine to compute by successive differences and set type for mathematical tables. His first model consisted of 96 wheels and 24 axes, later to be reduced to 18 wheels and 3 axes.

By 1822 Babbage proposed to his own government that they support his effort and in 1823 funds were set aside for this project. Frustration and inefficiency led to the termination of the monies and after eight years of steadfast attention to this venture, the British government abandoned Babbage claiming that the completion of the machinery would be too expensive. In total, the equivalent of $74,800 of government monies and $26,400 of Babbage's had been consumed. It seems clear that Babbage had made two major miscalculations: First, the construction of his Difference Engine would have cost about fifty times more money than he was given; second, he needed about two tons of novel brass, steel and pewter clockwork made to order, since it was not readily available in his day.

In addition to the design for the Difference Engine, which was to perform a limited set of operations, Babbage worked on his Analytical Engine which was to perform all arithmetic calculations and could combine such operations together to solve any conceivable arithmetic problem.

Although some years later Scheutz, a Swedish inventor, built a smaller working model of Babbage's machine, it was the latter who must be credited with the initial work in this area.

He had shaped and predicted many things to come. Babbage's work was finally recognized, one day in 1944, long after death, when the British magazine *Nature* noted the completion of Harvard University's Mark I computer as "Babbage's Dream Come True." The director of the Mark I project said: "If Babbage had lived seventy-five years later, I would have been out of a job."[6]

Electronic calculators were soon developed, and were marvels of speed. What was needed was a rapid way of feeding in information and recording it equally quickly when the calculation was made. The U.S. Bureau of the Census had been long concerned with this problem and a young statistician, Herman Hollerith, came to its assistance. For the 1890 census, he introduced the original ideas for using punched cards as a prime source of input and output of the population data. Ever since, the U.S. government has utilized the mechanical calculator for all of its major analyses.

Before the modern-day computer could be conceptualized, it was necessary to devise a way of symbolically handling statements that were either true or false. When Boolian algebra* became sophisticated, circuit designers began to utilize this powerful tool in developing suitable avenues for machine operations. The Bell Telephone Laboratories under the guidance of George Stibitz perfected a simple relay computer in 1938 that was capable of performing arithmetic operations on two complex numbers. The seed was planted and ready to sprout.

This landmark in history was followed by the Mark I, also known as the IBM-Harvard Mark I. Construction started in 1939 and was completed five years later in 1944. This partially self-directing machine could add two twenty-three digit numbers in three-tenths of a second, multiply them in five and seven-tenths seconds, or divide them in fifteen and three-tenths seconds.

Mark II was twelve times faster than Mark I, and Mark III

---

* The logic of computer design can be traced to George Boole, an English mathematician, who in 1854 proposed a two-valued algebra in logic theory. For every situation, there is a class and also a not-class; this is the concept of 1 and 0.

was the first to utilize magnetic tape and a magnetic drum memory that was completely electronic and operated with vacuum tubes (similar to the old radio tubes) for its mathematical computations.

The Second World War was a powerful force in advancing the state of technology in the computer field. In 1942, members of the faculty at the University of Pennsylvania conceived of the Electronic Numerical Integrator and Calculator (ENIAC), which was to become the first electronic computer when completed in 1947. It was used by the Ballistic Research Laboratories of the Ordnance Department until 1958. International Business Machines was beginning to move ahead in this new field; in 1948 it constructed the Selective Sequence Electronic Calculator (SSEC). This unit was 100 times faster than the Mark I. In 1950 at Los Alamos, SSEC performed nine million mathematical operations in 150 hours—the equivalent of a man's working something like 1,500 years, or about 90 working lifetimes. SSEC was scrapped in 1952. In this same year IBM (by now their initials were as famous as their full title) made their 701 commercially feasible. This machine could perform eight million computations in just a few minutes. Remington Rand introduced UNIVAC (Universal Automatic Computer), which was the first machine to be mass-produced. Their first unit was delivered to the Bureau of the Census in 1950 and, in the tradition of machine obsolescence, is now on display at the Smithsonian Institution in Washington, D.C.

There are two general types of computers—analog and digital. Analog computers measure quantities and digital computers count them. An analog computer is designed primarily to deal with "continuous mathematics," as illustrated by the slide rule. A digital computer is designed primarily to deal with "discrete mathematics," as illustrated by the abacus.

The more popular of the two, the digital computer, is composed of four basic components: the processing element that performs all the logical and mathematical operations; the memory, which stores the information and a list of the operations to be carried out; the input component, which enters data into the computer; and the output component, which distributes the data taken from the computer. These components enable the machine to remember, process and communicate.

A computer program is a list of instructions that tells the machine what operations to discharge. The computer functions by taking an instruction from its memory, reading it, obtaining the information requested, performing the necessary operations and obtaining the next instruction as directed by a previous instruction. A program can link together many such operations in sequence and cause the computer to perform an elaborate procedure with enormous speed.

The fact that the computer is a tool that remembers has tremendous implications. Since it can do an outstanding job of recording, it is expected that the computer will shortly replace writing as the principal means of storing information, at least in the United States. Computer memories of the future will probably be the bank of many forms of data including books, diagrams, graphs, drawings, and records of the many forms of art and music.

In the future, should a student want to study in detail the structure of the Empire State Building, he would merely go to his console at school (or perhaps at home) which connects to the Library of Congress. He would formally make known his request and, at the press of a button, a three-dimensional copy of the skyscraper would be projected on a screen before him. He could request that the picture come closer to him, to have only a small portion of the thirty-eighth floor appear. He would see on the screen an image which he can duplicate and keep as a permanent record.

The computer is also a powerful instrument for communication. Computers are designed to work with languages, symbols or graphic models. In the future, and even to some extent today, the routine aspects of business and government can be transacted by computers communicating with each other.

Machine translation has become an important application of the computer to linguistics. The problem in converting one language into another is that languages rarely follow any systematic pattern. Idioms are irregular and sentence structures are often illogical.

The problem of translating English to Russian and vice

versa is still a formidable one. On May 7, 1960, Khrushchev gave a speech to the Supreme Soviet of the U.S.S.R. which was reported the next day in *Pravda*. The machine translation came out this way:

> Comrade deputy! All appearing on session expressed full consent with/from positions, advanced in reports, and unanimous supported offer Soviet government about cancellation taxes with/from worker and employee and other measures, directed on increase welfare Soviet people, and about completion in 1960 year translation all worker and employee on abbreviated worker day. In own appearances deputy unanimous approved inside and foreign policy Soviet government.

The same passage, translated by a human, read:

> Comrade Deputies! All those who spoke at the session expressed complete agreement with the positions advanced in the reports, and unanimously supported the proposals of the Soviet government for abolition of taxes collected from industrial, office, and professional workers and for other measures directed at improving the welfare of the Soviet people, and for the completion in 1960 of the transition of all industrial, office, and professional workers to a shorter working day. In their speeches the deputies unanimously approved the internal and foreign policy of the Soviet government.[7]

   The first-generation computer contained a dazzling display of vacuum tubes that were expensive, inefficient and space-consuming. Consequently, the second-generation computer was built with transistorized panels that would enable smaller units of equal capability to be installed. It now had a unit of equal or superior size with capabilities ten times greater than its predecessor. The development of the transistor commenced in the early 1940s at the Bell Laboratories. Three physicists, later to become recipients of the 1956 Nobel Prize, produced a "point contact" transistor. To manufacture these devices for transferring signals, crystals of germanium and silicon are prepared with some impurities. Perhaps the most important application of the transistor has been the miniaturization of computer components.

Today, we are witnessing the third generation of computers which allow for greater speeds, capabilities and flexibility.

IBM's 360 system, introduced in the spring of 1964, is an example of this third generation. Its first generation was inaugurated with the vacuum tube 701. The 7070, a transistor machine, ushered in the second generation and now microelectronic circuits (miniaturized electronic circuits no larger than the head of a wooden match stick) of the 360 qualify, at least as far as IBM is concerned, as the third generation. Even now work is underway in IBM's laboratories on its fourth generation and possibly its fifth.

The chart on pages 90–91 identifies the four computer generations and how they differ:[8]

The IBM System 360, available in several models, includes nineteen combinations of speed and memory capacity. With these are forty-five types of auxiliary equipment. The model 90, their largest, has more than fifty times the power of the model 20, the smallest; this makes the model 90 the most powerful computer of its kind. The System 360 model is 100 times faster than the second-generation 7090 and can operate up to 8 million additions or 5 million multiplications every second, providing the kind of decision-making data that can be used to run an organization. Control Data Corporation's 7600 computer is considered to be the world's most powerful system.

During the early days of the computer, speed was measured in "microseconds" (millionths of a second). Computer speeds, between 1955 and 1965, increased by a factor of 200, from 25,000 additions per second to 5 million per second. In the period ending in 1975, speeds will increase another 200 times, allowing additions at the rate of a billion each second ("nanoseconds"). There are even engineering Trojans talking about measuring speeds of "picoseconds" (trillionths of a second).

In general, we can say that the present-day assets of the computer fall into four categories:

1. *Memory and storage:* The ability of the computer to collect and maintain an enormous amount of data to serve

the organization—ranging anywhere from hundreds of millions to billions of characters.

2. *Speed:* Thanks in great part to the transistor, speeds can be determined in the range of millionths or billionths of a second.

3. *Time-Sharing:* An innovation of the early 1960s, closely identified with third-generation computers, which permits many people access to the system without any appreciable delay.

4. *Real-Time:* The ability of a computer system to provide an answer almost immediately.

To discharge its responsibility, the computer must be told what to do. Therefore a "language" is needed that is intelligible to the computer. English must be translated into a form that will enable the electronic circuitry to operate effectively.

Some languages for computers are ALGOL, AUTOCODER, CALINT, FORTRAN, COBOL, GECOM, FLOWMATIC and JOVIAL. These represent the state of the art in which man adjusts to the machine's language capability. It will be years before the machine learns man's way of communicating. Of the many languages available for computer programs, the most popular is FORTRAN (formula translation), used mainly in IBM systems. The beauty of FORTRAN is that it is a program that does not require any knowledge of machine language.

Another major language, Common Business Oriented Language or COBOL, was developed as a direct result of a meeting held in 1958. The federal government had urged the evolution of a standard language for business data-processing, and called a meeting of computer manufacturers and users to clarify the situation. COBOL, an outgrowth of this effort, describes data in a standardized form through a stylized English. There was little initial interest in COBOL until 1962 when the Defense Department announced that it would only consider for purchase computer systems that could utilize COBOL.

The proliferation of languages (there are over 1,700) has created a variety of problems, one of which is very central to the success of data banks. Specific languages tend to make

Computer Generation	Some Distinguishing Technical Features	Systems Approach	Level of Systems	Benefits	Environment Required
1ST GENERATION (1955–1960)	• Vacuum tubes • Punched cards • Limited magnetic core • Machine language coding	• Conversion of existing applications	• Accounting • Clerical	• Savings in personnel displacement • Absorption of future work load due to expansion • Increased accuracy • Procedurization	• Pioneering attitude • Procedurization • Knowlege of existing methods • Investment in new tools
2ND GENERATION (1960–1965)	• Transistors • Magnetic tape • Expanded magnetic core • Symbolic languages including COBOL	• Segments of new management information system • Management science applications	• Technical • Middle management support • Operating management control	• Use of techniques not previously practical • Restructuring of information systems • Supplement to management's analytical capacity	• Willingness to use existing systems in new ways • People who can analyze abstract problems • Higher order techniques

3RD GENERATION (1965)	• Micro-monolithic circuitry • Disk storage • Real-time and time-sharing capability • Operating systems	• Large-scale systems • Logistics applications • Company-wide systems • Total systems approaches	• Management planning and analysis • Corporate headquarters coordination	• Interlocking of sub-systems • Vertical and horizontal extension of computer use • Speed	• High level competency in systems design and computer programming • Willingness to change local ways for company good • Long term, heavy investment
4TH GENERATION (*early* 1970s)	• Significant simplification of systems and programming analysis • Increased reliability • Increased flexibility • Confidentiality	• Extension of vital decision-making process	• Top management planning and decision-making	• Sharpening of most vital element of organization	• Rigorous analysis of top management functions • Business research • Availability of high level management systems analysts • Willingness to make vital changes

the purchaser of a system dependent on one manufacturer over a period of years. When conversion to another system is attempted, problems of compatibility become evident; i.e., a language developed for one machine is not acceptable to another unit. This need for making languages compatible would increase the cost of combining twenty different systems into one federal data bank.

These computer languages are written in a "binary" code. Unlike decimal numbers, which are built on a base of 10, binary numbers are on a base of 2. Using the base 10, when a digit is placed one space to the left and a zero is added, the number is worth 10 times as much as the original number. With binary numbers, each time a base number 2 is moved to the left, it is worth 2 times as much; that is, the number has increased by the power of 2. Therefore, while decimals increase on the order of 1, 10, 100, 1000, etc., binary numbers increase on the order of 1, 2, 4, 8, 16, 32, etc.

The other major concept of the binary code is that only 2 symbols are used in the system—1 and 0. Symbols 2 through 9 are never employed. The following comparison will explain the difference.

Decimal		Binary
00001	=	00001
00002	=	00010
00003	=	00011
00004	=	00100
00005	=	00101
00006	=	00110
00007	=	00111
00008	=	01000
00009	=	01001
00010	=	01010
.		.
.		.
.		.
00025	=	11001

Each digit in a binary number, either 1 or 0, is referred to as a *bit*. Data moves through the computer a *bit* at a time. This breakdown is necessary because the basic electronic parts of a computer usually exist in two possible states: 0 or 1— current is off or on, a switch is closed or open, a card is not

punched or is punched, a relay is broken or free flowing, etc.*
Once one of the computer languages previously discussed has
been converted to binary, it can then enter the computer's
memory as electronic pulses.

Most high-speed computers contain memory devices using
magnetic cores. These are minute "doughnuts" the size of
pinheads, which are made of a ferro-magnetic ceramic material. Each core can, at any one time, be magnetized in one
of two directions. Therefore, one direction stands for a binary
0; the other for a binary 1. Since these cores are arranged in
columns, any binary number can be stored.

Each column is assigned an address and can store either
one fact or one instruction. For example, if we tell the computer to read the contents of address 101, it will read each
of the cores in the column designated 101, moving the bits of
information in the form of electronic pulses, at the rate of
186,300 miles per second (the speed of light), to whatever
location is designated. Information is instantly "read out" of
any address and used in problem-solving. As desired, data can
be erased from any address and replaced with new information.

In 1968 National Cash Register introduced its third-generation computer system, the Century 100. NCR's technological
innovation is its memory unit. Instead of conventional dough-
nut-type cores, thin-film rods are used. Each rod, one-tenth
of an inch in length, is covered with a layer of magnetic
material and then "danced" into coils of wire where 4,600 rods
group together to make up a memory plane. Not only does this
advance suggest the future means of storing data, but it
will allow a less expensive way to manufacture memory units.

All systems today require an intermediate physical means
of communicating with the computers. There are nearly a
dozen ways, including punched cards, punched paper tapes,
magnetic tapes, magnetic disks and optical scanners.

The punched card, developed in 1880 by Dr. Herman
Hollerith, head of the Bureau of the Census' tabulating section,
contains 80 vertical columns; it can retain 80 characters of
information.

The punched paper tape is cheap and easily stored in rolls.

* There are some trinary systems that employ (−), (o) and (+), referring to minus, zero and plus.

Standard business equipment, i.e., specially designed typewriters and bank cash registers, are able to automatically
punch these tapes in a normal business operation.

The main recording medium for computer data today is the
magnetic tape. It retains a huge quantity of information. A
single 10½ inch reel can hold the contents of 250,000 punch
cards. In addition, tapes can be read at fantastic speeds: Only
1,200 characters a second can be read from punch cards, while
some computers read 120,000 characters or more from magnetic tapes.

The magnetic disk is fast becoming a principal form for
retaining data. It is easily stored and looks like a large phonograph record. The disks are placed one on top of another in
a pack; brushes then read from both sides of the disk at once.

A laser memory system has recently been designed by the
Precision Instrument Company in Palo Alto, California. Employing a single-watt, continuous-wave argon laser, bits of
information can be more readily recorded and retrieved than
with older methods. Traditional magnetic tapes contain about
5,600 bits of information per inch; the laser process yields
645,000 bits per inch. In addition, 12 million character bits
can be recorded each second.

Utilizing present laser technologies alone, a one-inch tape
of 4,800 feet could hold approximately twenty double-spaced
typed pages on every American citizen. The time required to
pull out data on a specific individual would be about four
minutes.

Consequently, a room of roughly 15 feet by 20 feet could
contain 100 tapes yielding 2,000 pages on every man, woman
and child in this country. The time required to retrieve a file
on a particular individual out of our population of 200 million
would be about ten minutes.

Photochromism, the ability of some materials to change
color under different kinds of light, is being researched for
possible use in storing at least 100 to 10,000 times as much
data as can be stored in a given computer memory area today.

:

The growth of the computer industry is quite staggering
to the imagination. From 1956 through 1968, installations grew

from 810 to more than 70,000. Most have been installed since 1965 and in fact almost 15,000 were installed in 1968 alone. The cumulative value of computer equipment installed has risen from $8 billion in 1965 to $12.5 billion in 1966 to more than $20 billion in 1968. Of the computer systems now in existence, more than two-thirds are used for general administrative and business purposes and, according to the 1967 issue of *Computers and Automation*, are applied in over 1,200 different ways.[9]

In Western Europe, Germany leads with installations and orders, totaling nearly 5,000; the United Kingdom is second with 2,113; and France is third with 1,715. The Benelux countries, Belgium, The Netherlands and Luxembourg, total 1,350 installations. By 1970 Western Europe's total should be at least 30,000.

In the United States, the computer has entered nearly every large organization; the variety of its functions is astounding. The Sheraton Corporation of America uses a Teleregister Computer to assist in making reservations in most of their chain's ninety hotels. The Reservatron is a system that allows the Sheraton Hotel organization to check available space and book guests in less than ten seconds.

A Cleveland department store, the Higbee Company, uses a computer and optical scanner in reading and processing sales checks. As customers make purchases, sales clerks write pertinent information on punched-card sales checks; these are used for all types of transactions—cash, C.O.D. and time-payment accounts. The sales checks are collected and scanned by a computer after the store closes.

In another application in business, it is possible now to pinpoint just what kind of products consumers use in any area, large or small. For example, one could locate the residences of every owner of a car of any make and year, so that car manufacturers could actually assign dealers or change franchises to keep up with potential demand. Or, for a product sold door-to-door, one could map the specific route the salesperson should follow.

In a report titled "Private Eye for Colorado,"[10] it was announced that Colorado will be the first state to use an automatic data-input system. Its department of revenue will add an optical scanner to its computer installation at Denver. The system will read standard typewritten print at the rate of 2,000 characters per second and will eliminate the manual preparation of punch cards for input. It was initially used for processing motor vehicle registration, but can be applied to driver history records, drivers' licenses, automobile titles and numerous tax purposes.

Computers are used to authorize credit purchases at the point-of-sale. Before a transaction is made, a computer will scan the consumer's records to determine his ability to purchase. Obviously, this has to be done quickly, conveniently and without embarrassment to the consumer. The system has to be designed not to introduce an annoying or undignified note into the transaction, or one inconsistent with the image the retailer is trying to create. Not giving the impression of an impersonal and arbitrary refusal to authorize a purchase is obviously something of concern to store managers.

Touch-tone shopping will soon be available to the housewife, thanks to the computer. The Bell Telephone System predicts that in the future the housewife will possess account cards for numerous stores. When she sees items she wants in an ad or a catalog, she calls the store and gets back a signal that the computer is ready to receive. She inserts her card, transmitting her account number, and taps out the items' codes (as printed in the ad or catalog) and the quantities she desires. The information is recorded directly onto the machine for processing through credit, inventory, shipping and billing. The housewife will also be able to pay bills at any time of day or night without writing checks, addressing envelopes or licking stamps. She calls her bank's computer and her card tells it her personal checking-account number and the amounts of her payments. The computer debits her account and credits the account of each store. If she overdraws, the computer can warn her and (depending upon its own internal instructions from the bank's manager, who could even be vacationing at this point) extend credit to her account.

Department stores have long been users of computers. The Grayson-Robinson apparel chain, which operates more than a hundred stores throughout the nation, receives tapes daily from its outlets. The information is converted into punch cards enabling the merchandise and inventory-control function to be calculated on its computer. Sixty per cent of the sales data for any one week is received and summarized by computers. On the Monday morning after, the remaining 40 per cent of the sales data is incorporated, and the computer system begins running style reports. These reports are run up by department and price line in order to obtain the necessary merchandising data. The entire massive operation is terminated by Wednesday afternoon of each week, including reports on all inactive stockpiles.

Games with computers are one way of looking at the business world without taking all the risks. MARKISM, a business game for marketing decision, was developed by two professors at Pennsylvania State University. The marketing manager is faced—in a make-believe situation called simulation—with decisions about price and quality of product, national advertising, retailers' advertising allowances, the industry's market potentials, and competitors' decisions. Consumer demand is a function of many factors; the manager is taught the relation among these factors and the way the relation changes with the product, the company and the market. The computer evaluates the players' marketing strategy in light of the progress of the competition.

The computer has become an integral part of Wall Street. Merrill Lynch, Pierce, Fenner & Smith, a major investment house, conducted a massive computerized examination of rates of return on common stock. Bond Trade Analysis Program is an IBM effort enabling a bank to identify the net dollars-and-cents effects of trading on its bond holdings. Another activity simulates the investment-trust process.

The computer has even been used to solve problems of scholarship. The authorship of fifteen of the essays in *The Federalist* has been in question. A computer at M.I.T. was able to determine which of the papers were written by James Madison, and which by Alexander Hamilton. To accomplish this feat the writing of the two men had to be catalogued to identify patterns for each; then these were matched with the documents. The result was that, of the fifteen papers, Madison was credited with eleven; the probability was 80 to 1 that he also authored the twelfth; it was determined that two documents were written with Hamilton; and the last paper still could not be identified as having the imprint of either statesman.

Using more than 100,000 interviews gathered from election opinion polls between 1952 and 1960, a computer was used to predict voter reaction to candidate John F. Kennedy in 1960. Three months prior to the Presidential election the computer had accurately predicted the outcome.

Computers are also at work in the transportation industry. A UNIVAC system installed in the Toronto City Hall is coupled with 2,000 automatic traffic sensors placed underground. These sensors detect and measure the density and direction of traffic flow along major arteries and feed this information to the computer system. The computer absorbs this continuous flow of traffic data and analyzes it, intersection by intersection, several times each second. Corrective signals are sent out simultaneously to a thousand traffic lights throughout the city. The result is a 38 per cent faster flow of traffic in Toronto.

Photogrammetry, already a construction tool of the aerospace industry, is now being perfected for use by auto companies. A clay mock-up of a new car model is photographed in three dimensions. The pictures are translated into a code for punched tape; the tape is then fed into equipment that does all the work formerly done by die- and template-makers and draftsmen.

Other transportation agencies are moving quickly toward computerized operation. The New York Central (now Penn Central Railroad) installed the first computer-fed TV units that retrieve instant data on the location of any of the 125,000 freight cars on its 10,000 miles of track.

A competitor of the railroads has moved rapidly in this field. Probably the most famous example is the American Airlines installation. A $30.5 million SABRE system gives instant up-to-the-minute data about every plane seat and reservation in any of its ticket offices.

Computer assistance is at work for the United States Lines and Moore-McCormack shipping freight service. For example, on the *American Racer*, a computer helps the captain steer and control the engine from the ship's bridge. Prior to the use of computers 51 men were needed; now the ship's work force has been reduced to 39. Thus on land, in the air and on the sea computers are found in operation.

A computer is now used in the hiring of dock workers on the waterfront of New York City. Locked in the files of two IBM 360 models are lists of all dock workers. "By using leased telephone wires, the computers are connected with fifty-six input and output units located in the thirteen hiring centers maintained by the Waterfront Commission. . . . Hiring agents utilize IBM port-a-punch cards, one for each gang and one for each dock list—but not to exceed twenty-five men per card—which are inserted into the input units at the appropriate times to transmit information on hiring to the computer, where it is recorded and stored. The next day, at the casual hiring stage, dock workers who are seeking employment insert their plastic 'seniority badges' into the input units (i.e., they 'badge in') and the information is transmitted to the computer. As a man inserts his badge, there is an instantaneous checking by the computer of its memory, followed by immediate transmission of eligibility information to the output unit which, within five or six seconds, types a slip for the waiting dock worker."[11]

The McLouth Steel Corporation in Detroit has in operation a computer-controlled rolling mill. Costing $3 million, the computer gives instructions regarding 83 different grades of steel in 47 sizes and reduces scrap waste by 1½ per cent.

American Electric Power System employs computers to determine the movement of generators in its fifteen plants in six states. When there is an increased demand for power, its central computer in Ohio automatically weighs the cost of fuel for each plant, the transmitting power cost and the efficiency ratio, and then determines which plant should release the extra energy power.

Computers have also found their way into the New York Bar Association. Recently this legal organization staged a mock trial at which it subpoenaed computerized business files as evidence. Questions were raised about how to cross-examine a computer, and whom to blame when a machine's conclusion caused a corporation to run afoul of antitrust laws.

The list of computer applications appears to be endless.

They are found working in the most unlikely areas—such as religion—in a variety of applications. The Dead Sea Scrolls were deciphered by scholars using computers. During the recent Ecumenical Council held in St. Peter's Basilica in Rome, computers were used to count ballots. The church utilizes computers in adapting to modern spiritual needs. During the winter of 1968, in a Roman Catholic monastery near St. Louis, a computer was used to provide a 71-facet view of each practicing Catholic. A Honeywell 1200 computer was installed in Nashville in the spring of 1968 to help design a new Sunday-school curriculum—including hymns—offered by the Southern Baptist Convention's 34,000 churches.

In attempting to solve a Biblical mystery, two scholars noted that of the twenty-one Pauline epistles found in the New Testament, the first fourteen, from Romans and Hebrews, were attributed to the Apostle Paul. After several hundred years of debate, Biblical researchers decided to determine the truth. Using 400 samples of Greek prose texts of 600,000 words taken from twelve authors, they were able to identify seven accurate tests of authorship. "We discovered by applying with the help of our computer the seven tests of authorship, that each one gave the same result. Five of the fourteen Epistles were indistinguishable: Romans first and second Corinthians, Galatians, and Philemon. The remaining nine came from at least five other hands." Paul was accepted as the author of Galatians, therefore these five were the real epistles. (The chronological order of Plato's work was also determined in a similar fashion.)

Even the arts are being affected. A computer was able to write poems in California by relating a 3,500 word vocabulary to 128 patterns of simple sentences. Here is an example:

> *Few fingers go like narrow laughs.*
> *An ear won't keep few fishes,*
> *Who is that rose in that blind house?*
> *And all slim, gracious blind planes are coming,*
> *They cry badly along a rose,*
> *To lead is stuffy, to crawl was tender.*

A *Time* magazine review commented: "Faced with this poem, any competent modern critic could easily go to work. He might first allude to its use of alliteration ('few fishes,' 'few fingers'). Clearly the poem deals with the plight of modern man reaching out for love and innocence but mocked by impending death. Love is the rose stifling in the blind house of modern technology. Note the repeated theme of blindness, and the plane that will bring annihilation to the world. Like the world, human love has no future. And little religious comfort. (The fish was an early symbol of Christian faith, now reduced—hence 'few fishes.') Mirth, too, has shrunk to 'narrow laughs,' though the poet, like Western man himself, fondly recalls the lost gentleness of childhood ('to crawl was tender')." The reviewer concluded that the computer time cost $100,000, so the resulting poem could not be called free verse.[12]

Computers have been used to analyze the accuracy of 2,000 claimed UFO's (unidentified flying objects). To date, the study has been narrowed down to only three sightings supported by ample photographic or eyewitness evidence. The first, made in Oregon in 1950, was a farmer's photograph of a saucer 20 to 30 feet in diameter. The second sighting took place in Texas in 1957, where glowing elliptical objects 200 feet long crossed highways. The third case was in Brazil in 1958, where scientific personnel aboard a Brazilian navy ship spotted a Saturn-shaped UFO and photographed it four times. This series of pictures was analyzed electronically for authenticity with the help of a computer.

New applications are being pushed on the market every month. The Raytheon Company has an automated, mobile classroom that teaches driver-education by using a computer to monitor student performance. The computer immediately tells the driver what action he should take when he deviates from good driving technique.

For the more than 5 million devotees of, and 40 million dabblers in, astrology in the United States, a computer program is available to prepare personal horoscopes. In the past it might have taken one full week and $500 to determine a person's entire astrological profile. The TBS Computer Centers Corporation and Time Pattern Research, Inc., now have a program that can produce a 10,000-word personal astrological analysis and forecast in one minute, based on an individual's name, sex and precise time of birth.

Bradshaw Realty uses a computer to match potential roommates on the basis of their personality traits, living patterns, interests and finances. A charge of $15 is made for the roommate-matching service, and another $15 for finding the appropriate place to live. Each applicant is given the names of at least six persons likely to be congenial. Then the roommates can interview each other to make their final choices.

Despite the effectiveness of these varied applications of computers, occasionally there are mistakes. One such incident occurred recently in the Army Reserves' computerized data bank in St. Louis where some two hundred New York State Reservists were ordered to two weeks' active duty in Wisconsin—which came as a complete surprise to the Pentagon.

A disaster resulted when a computer programmer at Cape Kennedy omitted a hyphen between two fives on his punch card: The computer's instructions were misread and the rocket, shaking off course, started to Rio de Janeiro. Less than five minutes after lift-off, the rocket, which cost over $18 million, had to be destroyed in mid-air.

A computer was rented by co-owners of the Food Center Wholesale Grocers in Boston to inventory their 4,500 items and reduce labor costs. Manpower was cut, but the inventory control became a total mess. Instead of peaches, oranges were delivered; an order for twelve cases of soup resulted in delivery of 240 cases; an order for napkins brought toilet tissues. Computerized billing for $14 was sent out as $214; some grocers were overcharged while others received no bills for merchandise supplied. The Food Center sued the computer manufacturer and received a court award for $53,200 in damages.

The vulnerability of the computer was indicated at the New York Stock Exchange where the $6 million computer-fed ticker tape broke down for three and a half hours because of a loophole in the process by which their most sophisticated computer ordinarily detected errors in punch cards feeding the ticker tape new information. Luckily, in this particular case, there was an alternative—switching to the old method of recording stock transactions by hand.

The Senate Subcommittee on National Security and International Relations is concerned about the Pentagon's reliance on its 3,225 computers. Senators were primarily anxious that some military decisions were made by computer operators and that results printed out from the computers were often accepted more readily by the military than were dissenting opinions of skilled personnel.

:

The computer idea has become so popular that do-it-yourself computer centers are growing. In Chicago there is a computer service that allows customers to drive in and process information, much as a housewife drives to a laundromat. Called Data-Mat, the service permits a customer to bring unprocessed data to a midtown center, obtain free parking, use a private office to prepare information and perform all necessary computations on any of four computer systems. The center is open around the clock, seven days a week, with attendants available at all times to assist customers.

There is a way to give obsolete computers a "second chance." Computer System Leaseback salvages computers. The comparison with the automobile market is obvious and quite valid; the residual value of an automobile at the end of its product-life has long been recognized, and has created the important used-car business. Use of "used" computers grows as new arrangements are conceived to meet the needs of the market—it is a valuable alternative to purchasing or renting the most up-to-date equipment, which for many is too expensive. These "used" computers can often be bargains for the purchaser, even though they may be slower and somewhat less efficient than their newer counterparts. In 1962 a UNIVAC I that had been in operation for three years was returned to Sperry Rand. The manufacturer reconditioned the model and sold it for one-tenth of its original price, which was $1 million.

On the other hand, should an organization wish to stay away from both expensive new equipment and older machines, it has the option of utilizing a service bureau, which is geared to handling massive projects from a great many companies. The client is assured the use of the latest equipment and, perhaps most important, he need not get bogged down with installing and making operational his own system. Service bureaus have become a major industry in this country.

They operate either as independents or as sub-units of computer manufacturers. By 1964 there were 600 service centers throughout the United States.

In addition, computers are being used to evaluate the success or failure of other computer installations. Donald J. Herman, president of COMPRESS, Inc., has a novel package called SCERT (Systems and Computer Evaluation and Review Technique). Through a variety of techniques, SCERT can predetermine the effectiveness of computers in any given situation; this information is invaluable to management when it chooses equipment. SCERT is an extremely complex and fairly large program, containing 31,000 instructions. It maintains a library of approximately 100,000 pieces of information. A complete service analysis takes about four weeks.

The form and application of computers are changing radically. Now they have such power, can store so much information and process it so quickly that it becomes possible to "time-share" one computer. Time-sharing means literally that many people have access to the single computer installation. The computer is so capable and rapid that it creates the illusion that each user has his own computer. Those who employ a time-shared computer can be thousands of miles away from the complex. All that is required is a telephone connection to a remote electric typewriter-like device. Earlier examples of this time-sharing included the local stock brokerage and airline reservation systems. In one system, over 3,000 stockbrokers around the nation can push a few buttons to display the latest prices on any selected stock. Placing and confirming an airline reservation in a matter of seconds is now common practice.

Dr. Louis Rader, Vice-President of General Electric Co., said, "Time-sharing on a computer is similar to playing a Steinway piano in the privacy of your own home, compared to playing one in Carnegie Hall. You have the chance to make your own mistakes and learn to play at your own speed. You also have the blessings of a big computer on the occasional big problem without being stuck with big costs of a big computer or the limitation of a small computer. In this sense, time-sharing is for everybody. It redistributes the wealth of computers among businessmen of every kind and size giving each one a piece of a big machine."[13]

The earlier data-processing systems were, and to a great extent still are, primarily concerned with the accounting function—payroll, billing, general accounting—or with scientific inquiry. Over the next several years major changes will improve the utilization of computers. There will be greater sophistication in dealing with more operating aspects of institutional life, e.g., production and inventory management, sales analysis, budget control, data banks. With the third generation of computers, newer systems are being unveiled to accompany those already in existence, leading to a totally integrated complex. The equipment in these installations will include a keyboard machine, central processor, operating memory, file storage and hard copy input. More advanced installations might possess a satellite processor, image processor, console display, screen and visual display and a hard copy output.

The recent development of scanners, or optical character-recognition devices (OCR), has opened up new horizons for the computer. Using a light beam for invoices, checks, credit cards, etc., a photosensitive receiver changes the reflected light directly into electrical impulses. At the home office of an oil company, a scanner reads over 10,500 cards each hour and can reject imperfect ones to be reviewed by hand. What used to take two weeks of daily operation is now done in one hour.

Optical scanners read utility bills, insurance forms, sales slips and numerous other completed paper forms; 1,800 typewritten words can be read with ease every minute. We will witness an increasing growth in the use of such recognition devices over the next few years.

IBM has an advanced communication technique that can double the speed at which their computers "talk" to each other by telephone. The technique, called Binary Synchronous Communications (BSC), is designed specifically for their model 360. Computers in this network may "talk," or exchange data, with other computers and devices across a city or a continent via telephone and private lines. Thus the user can respond rapidly to an event originating anywhere in his organization.

To integrate the system that will be of superior service to data banks, major evolutionary steps will be necessary. To begin with, the "main" computer will begin to play a relatively smaller role in the makeup of the overall system. Complementing the present capacity, three-dimensional pictures will begin to play a more important role. Advances in software, abstracting and indexing, memory technology communications, and graphic displays will be part of this future development.

All of these innovations are not presently available and barriers must be removed before they can be realized, probably in the 1970s. In this interim period, specific steps toward such a system will be made. When finally developed, the integrated system will find its initial application in large organizations, with the federal government as an immediate purchaser.

Between 1969 and 1970, the third generation of computer systems will become more commonplace and will gradually replace the current second-generation equipment. During this period, there will be introduction of information storage and retrieval systems, and digital-communication terminal equipment. Such terminals will be sophisticated typewriter-units (some with television screens) placed strategically throughout the country, with tielines to the central computer.

How does all this advancement assist in the creation of a more reliable and efficient data bank? One of the principal characteristics of the integrated systems in the period from 1969 to 1972 will be a substantial increase in cost effectiveness; this is a basic argument given by Civil Service Commissioner Macy for such a massive data bank. This saving will be most easily seen in the larger-scale systems, where the unit-cost per unit-measure is expected to be reduced by as much as 50 per cent.

The prime purpose of the integrated information system will be to perfect an institutional control over operations, and to provide data and techniques for better planning. The latest equipment will aid in the accomplishment of this objective; then the computer will have the power to keep track of just about any form of recordable data.

The computer is a useful device primarily because it can

solve math problems much faster than can a human being. But in order to utilize this speed advantage, it was necessary that the program be stored in the machinery in advance (rather than being fed, as required, in a step-by-step process by the operator). Thus, the realization of the computer had to wait for the appearance of a practical, large-capacity memory system in which to economically store, for immediate reference, extensive lists of instruction sequences. The development of magnetic-tape recording techniques and the invention of the magnetic drum and the ferrite core provided the memory elements that permitted the incredible computer development of the past decade.

:

What does all this suggest? One might say that, in a sense, we are talking about a computerized system that can handle one of the least-understood, most disconnected experiences in life—communications. With the latest innovations, we shall be able to send and receive enormous quantities of verbiage to be codified and classified as we see fit. With the expected continued growth and increased diversification not only of governmental institutions but of all others, these obstacles will continue to grow.

To date, most data-processing systems have been designed to meet the information requirements of only one part of the total organization. Typically, very little interchange of information takes place among the different departments of an institution. However, during the past few years there has been a growing appreciation of the need for using communication-oriented data-processing systems to obtain closer control and integration. This trend, which was brought about by technical advances in communication and data-processing equipment, promises to eliminate many of the shortcomings of current systems and greatly increase the total information capabilities of the organization.

There are many ways in which this sophistication is evolving. In the fall of 1968, at the Jet Propulsion Laboratory at Pasadena, California, a computer was installed that is able to detect its own malfunctions and actually repair itself. It was the first fully automatic, self-repairing computer ever built, and will carry out this function in addition to serving as a special-purpose computer.

Another sophistication that will come about before the end of the decade is the use of more and more leased lines of joint voice and data usage. There will be extensive use of closed-circuit television with computer control and information capability, and a limited use of group presentation displays. In addition, a limited introduction of private videophone equipment and limited speech recognition will be introduced; a multipurpose data station and optical-character recognition will be in general use. Although it is anticipated that the costs of this mechanization will be a limiting factor, the government will in all probability expend considerable resources to obtain this strength.

There will be innovations when fourth-generation computers appear in the early 1970s. Microprogramming, a system whereby the programmer uses the basic, built-in instructions of a computer to develop other instructions, is available in some equipment now.

Another predicted growth will be in the increased applications to computer memory of Cryogenics, a branch of physics relating to the production and effects of very low temperatures. When temperatures reach "absolute zero," the systems can perform at a more rapid and therefore more effective speed.

Laser beams will probably be useful in protecting against breakdowns in computers in the next decade. This process is known as polymorphism. Lasers will enable the computer to keep going, even if part of its circuitry breaks down. Instead of an instant falling-apart, there will be a series of failures over a period of time, allowing the most important circuitry to fail last.

What is already obvious is that the newest machines are easier to operate. More and more middle-level businessmen with little training will be able to utilize the equipment. In fact, plans are underway for computers to automatically feed data to appropriate specialists within an organization. It will not even be necessary for the specialist to request the information.

The fourth-generation computers of the coming decade will be built to function more and more like data banks, gradually moving from data processing to more information retrieval.

As the technology moves into the eighth decade of this century, it will develop an ability to communicate plans and policies effectively to those charged with implementing them. Not too dissimilar to the stereotype of the war rooms in the Pentagon, the management command function will be extended by using group presentation displays and videophones to improve individual-to-individual communications. Although large businesses and governments may have decentralized line and message computers, the system will ultimately be characterized as almost completely centralized, with computer control of all internal communications. Hence, a national data bank in a specific building will become feasible and practical.

According to Dr. Louis Rader, "The electronic computer may have a more beneficial potential for the human race than any other invention in history."[14] To be sure, no other single innovation of man has altered so many human activities in so short a time. In less than a decade and a half, the computer has profoundly changed the techniques of science and has begun to make the government more efficient.

Since information, quickly retrieved, is directly related to potential power and therefore an ability to manipulate and control, it is within the realm of possibility that the United States may have finally achieved the technological ability to be superior to any country in the world. We may achieve the godlike capability to have available, at the push of a button, the secrets of all nations; in fact, secrets unknown even to the nation they concern.

Technologically, a very sophisticated national data bank and worldwide data banks will be reliable and practical very soon. Memory speeds will have caught up with processing speeds, and speed and accuracy will have improved dramatically. As processing systems become more deeply involved in decision operations, leaders in all fields will become more intimately involved in asking for computer developments of information on an hour-to-hour basis. Then we will no longer have to question who commands the nation, or for that matter the world. The technology has responded to the wishes of its masters—and as for Babbage, certainly his dream has come true.

In accepting an honorary degree from the University of Notre Dame a few years ago, David Sarnoff of Radio Corporation of America said: "We are too prone to make technological instruments the scapegoats for the sins of those who wield them. The products of modern science are not in themselves good or bad; it is the way in which they are used that determines their value."[15]

CHAPTER VI

Along the Road to Psychological Submission

Today man lives in an atmosphere dominated by the machine. He brushes his teeth with an electric toothbrush; prepares his meals with mechanical toasters, oven and broilers; works in an atmosphere of motors, switches, fans, typewriters; goes to and from home by car, bus and train; reduces the chores of home life with sewing machines, washing machines and drying machines. In the past only the craftsman used the tool. Today all of us take machinery for granted. As long as machines served us and did not threaten our rights as persons, we welcomed technology.

The charm of the horse-drawn buggy yields to the modern automobile; the candlestick maker is not needed in this day of electric power; the complexities of the abacus are incorporated into the computer's memory unit. Often we are glad to say goodbye to what we leave behind because many innovations free man from monotony, physical effort and waste of energy.

Computerized data banks are a part of this advance, aiding

us in ways that are valuable for our everyday living and essential for progress on all levels. Much of what has been achieved in medical research and outer-space exploration would have been impossible without the wide range of sophisticated computers. Payroll accounting, statistical analysis and other administrative methods could not be carried on without their use. Military defense and corporate decision-making would be hampered while data piled up.

Unfortunately, sacrifices frequently accompany these changes. There may be displacements, obsolescence of skills and a need to alter the way in which we interact with the machine. According to the authors of *The Year 2000*, ". . . computers are likely to match, simulate, or surpass some of man's most 'human-like' intellectual abilities, including perhaps some of his aesthetic and creative capacities, in addition to having some new kinds of capabilities that human beings do not have."[1] In fact, at the University of Nebraska, researchers are employing computers to simulate emotions and feelings. A system was programmed to duplicate such emotions as love, fear and anger in varying situations of satisfaction, frustration and pain.

Computers have not only studied emotion, but have been put to work interpreting personality. A firm of management consultants, which specializes in the selection of sales personnel, believes human behavior is very easily categorized. This firm has introduced a completely automated process for preparing reports on sales candidates for its clients. Within this device are stored a number of standard paragraphs. A consultant makes his judgment regarding the referral and pushes a series of appropriate buttons. The machine automatically types out an evaluation report on the client. Since this typing machine has limits of memory capacity (approximately 1,000 paragraphs), the firm that uses it appears to believe that there are similar limits in human behavior. These methods imply a belief that it is possible to reduce to computerized form the total variability of motivations, abilities, temperamental qualities and environmental factors which influence success or failure in the sales profession. Moreover, this absurdly simplistic view of behavior is translated into a sales and advertising device that "guarantees" the sales success of the men to whom they give an "A" recommendation.

The Wall Street Journal, in its discussion of this impersonal-evaluation approach, wrote that this consulting firm " 'has developed . . . a system of administering aptitude tests by wire.' A company wishing to evaluate a job applicant can arrange to have a test administered in a local Western Union office. The test takes only fifty minutes to administer, is blindly interpreted without a psychologist having first hand information about the candidate; but this firm nevertheless claims that this test will 'select in advance those who will and those who will not be highly productive sales, service and managerial personnel.' "[2]

The Psychological Corporation sells a test called the Minnesota Multiphasic Personality Inventory (MMPI). Not only is the test scored mechanically, but a computer-based, clinical-interpretative analysis of personality is typed out and returned to the client without evaluation by a psychologist. It appears that this reputable company believes that clinical analysis of the subject by a psychologist can be replaced by a computer program. The criticism of "blind testing" (interpreting test scores without having interviewed or interacted with the client) has been overlooked; diagnostic terms are included in the evaluation without any knowledge of the person's background or environmental influences on him. This computer analysis of the MMPI is advertised in their 1967 catalogue, with no special warnings, instructions or cautions with regard to the use of these results. "A one-page report provides a computer printout of diagnostic and interpretive statements descriptive of the subject's personality, in addition to the scores and profile for the fourteen standard scales plus scores on eleven research scales and a special scale developed at the Mayo Clinic."[3] A qualified psychologist, therapist or counselor can purchase this service and use it in schools, hospitals, private practice or industry. When the subject has completed the MMPI, it is sent to the Psychological Corporation for evaluation by the computer, and returned by mail to the analyst. The service costs $3 for a single case and is reduced to $1.40 for 300 or more cases.

the splendid wonders of the computer we find
asking: Has man become submissive to the com-
today? Can each individual profess to be more human
tions than the complex system he has developed to
daily endeavors? Will there be a growing tendency
te a world where we treat each other as machines?
Are we building more barriers which prevent the individual
from having the opportunity to evolve his own unique potentials—to be self-realized?

Many people have fallen victim to an array of psychological
manipulations resulting from direct or indirect contact with
computers. The eminent psychoanalyst Erich Fromm warned,
in *The Sane Society*, that in the automated world the individual will do "nothing but watch some instrument and pull some
lever from time to time."[4]

Some researchers have concluded that the role of individual
creativity in the computerization process diminishes as the
technology gives the machine more decision-making responsibility.

Jacques Ellul, author of *The Technological Society*, believes
we are facing the greatest danger ever: the domination of
human life by technique—the theory that there is only one
best way to do anything. In his book, he reported a meeting
held in 1960 at which American and Russian scientists made
predictions about the year 2000: "Knowledge will be accumulated in 'electronic banks' and transmitted directly to the
human nervous system by means of coded electronic messages.
There will no longer be any need of reading or learning moun-
tains of useless information; everything will be received and
registered according to the needs of the moment. There will be
no need of attention or effort. What is needed will pass directly from the machine to the brain without going through
consciousness."[5]

Donald Michael, who coined the phrase "cybernation" to
describe the impact of cybernetics on society, envisioned the
individual swallowed up by computers and an ultimate alienation between government and citizen. In testimony before a
Congressional subcommittee, Dr. Michael said: "Even today,
many people are willing, indeed sometimes want to believe

that the behavioral scientist can understand and manipulate
their behavior . . . certainly the capacity for invasion will
increase as behavioral engineering increases . . . the systematic
exposure of the private self . . . is becoming steadily more
widespread and probably more acceptable."[6]

Man's submission to the machine was tested by sociologist
Robert S. Lee when he discovered widespread anxiety about
computers during interviews with 3,000 persons. He found
that the major concern was "the idea that there is some sort
of science fiction machine that can perform the functions of
human thinking . . . which engenders a feeling of inferiority
and has strong emotional significance for people."[7]

John Wilkinson at the Center for the Study of Democratic
Institutions in Santa Barbara believes that man has lost his
footing. Machines have set the pace and are running out of
control—the country is confronted with "the possibility of the
imminent destruction of all human values."[8]

Man submits more and more as his ability to make choices
about and control his future is taken gradually away from
him. He is willing to have the machine make numerous decisions for him about his future; he is willing to permit the
machine to build towers of brick and metal, hoping that it
will not fail him when he has to live or work in them; he is
willing to have the machine process his life's facts, hoping
that it will be accurate and objective. With the consolidation
of computer systems, according to Herman Kahn and Anthony
Wiener, ". . . control may pass from man to machines, in which
case, although population may be limited since it serves no
useful function, to the extent to which humankind is permitted
to persist it may be kept in a perpetually drugged and/or
subservient state. This would prevent rebellion and the dis-
turbance of other 'undesirable' interference. By determining
what information to feed back to the computer-linked con-
trollers and by manipulating the logic of the problem, the
computers may gradually gain control of the entire system."[9]

:

It seems that we are not aware of what is happening to us
—that we are losing a little each day to the machines. We are

usually too busy to think about matters which seem on the surface not to be so important as whether our cars are safe, or the price of bacon or the way taxes are skyrocketing.

Since World War I, psychologists have attempted to determine the impact of work on man. With the advent of automated and computer devices, they have expanded their research inquiries. Even in the study of traditional, non-computerized work situations, conclusions may at times be contradictory; therefore psychologists and other social scientists may be understandably even less certain of their findings as they survey the impact of computers on man.

The research in the field demonstrates a lack of certainty of what to look for, a lack of agreement on approaches for studying industrial change, and a lack of overall theory. The confusion along these lines is crystallized in Floyd Mann's statement describing studies in the advanced forms of technology as a "field rampant with speculation and unverified hypotheses."[10] The lack of a systematic approach has been questioned by Neil and William Smelser who said, ". . . scientific study of the relation between the individual and his social surroundings has scarcely begun."[11] If we are indeed becoming more and more submissive to a computerized world, we are still years behind in clearly stating, in a way that can be investigated, the problems that relate to submission. Norbert Wiener, the eminent M.I.T. professor (and coiner of the word *cybernetics*), served us this warning: "It is my thesis that machines can and do transcend some of the limitations of their designers and in doing so they may be both effective and dangerous."[12]

Problems confronting the researchers include the variety of methods used, and the sheer number of computer problems to be studied. Some of the organizational experts were more concerned with the mechanics of the changes than with their larger impact. Some have used interviews, others, questionnaires, and still others, observations, as their basis for judgment. However, many of these studies are limited by the lack of really comparable control groups. For example, it is not sufficient to observe and measure the reactions and changes of behavior of clerks, keypunchers or programmers, without matching the experimental group with a comparable one which has been followed similarly under a non-computerized working environment.

Another curious shortcoming—and it is a serious one—is that people may not accurately perceive the changes of which they are part. Einar Hardin and Gerald Hershey attempted to determine whether employees can see changes in their work situations. The specific factor checked was whether employees in one insurance firm noted the presence or absence of change in the salary received several months prior to the investigation. Twenty-seven per cent of the respondents, a significant number, gave incorrect reports on what pay they had actually received. The authors raise the question, To what extent can we rely on the accuracy of employees' ability to perceive change? Their conclusions of this study raise doubts about the value of using questionnaires.[13] Merely asking workers how they are affected by computers may be of little value, since they are often not consciously aware of the interaction, in either a negative or positive way. Questions about how you like your new job in this computer center, or how happy you are now that certain work is done by a computer, may reveal little in terms of the way in which the machine is making inroads on you as a human being.

The way employees react to computers is influenced by their experiences prior to working on the computerized job. Professor Lawrence Williams of Cornell's School of Industrial and Labor Relations points out that there is evidence showing that the "human element in an organization will react to change in terms of how the last one was handled."[14] How the employer oriented and prepared his workers for the expected change; how extensive the changes were; whether there were layoffs in anticipation of the computer; whether they took place in an old structure or a new building in a new location —these are all factors. If the transition is gradual, or smoothly introduced, the impact may be minimal, although just because the changeover is orderly, does not mean it has no effect on the personality. Certainly, when the worker walks in one morning to a completely different work environment, there is justification for concern.

Those who work with computers appear to find their jobs

quite dull. In a survey of nineteen firms utilizing computers, Ida R. Hoos reported that the workers said their new jobs were dull.[15] There was more interest in the previous job, since it included alternately filing, checking, posting and typing. The employees now complained of being tied to a machine. Moving out of a general office into a computer-center operation meant no upgrading in skills. The workers lost what few opportunities they had to demonstrate initiative and judgment, since the work on key-punch machines and the like was thoroughly simplified and yet called for extreme speed and accuracy.

A report issued by the Organization for Economic Cooperation and Development in 1961 suggested that automation was beginning to make the office appear more and more like a factory.[16] Since computers operate best in structured situations, the casual or "whenever you want" coffee break and small talk are on the way out.

The need for speed and closer attention to the machine's operation produces the same kind of boredom one finds in factories. As more white-collar workers think about their similarity with blue-collar factory workers, they will feel a gradual loss of status. Walter Buckingham tells of an automated Coca-Cola inspection line that was so boring that an occasional 7-Up bottle was inserted to keep the inspectors from falling asleep.[17]

The efficiency with which it is used may determine how the computer affects the employee. The computer requires changes in the worker's performance. A person working under the influence of a computer feels the need for increased accuracy because it is now easier to detect errors and attribute them to a specific individual. According to Williams, "The anonymity of many office jobs is removed and a person's performance becomes very visible."[18] Then, too, an efficient, integrated, computer system demands that one do certain things at certain times. There are pressures for meeting deadlines. This in turn greatly affects the pace of work and reduces the possibility of "goofing off," or bending from a tight schedule. There is evidence that what we are so blithely giving in to under the influence of computers is precisely what we have been trying to replace in factories—unpleasant working conditions. Ida

Hoos, in her study of electronic data computers in twenty firms in San Francisco, found that "work is more routine, monotonous, pressured, and confining for the clerical workers involved."[19] She adds that there is now a factory-like, depersonalized atmosphere, heat from the key-punch machines, increased measurement of work and the introduction of shift work. She found still further loss of autonomy with increased centralization of functions from branch offices. In addition, there were poorer advancement opportunities, which affected many of the employees adversely.

Another way in which computers are beginning to make work more factory-like is that they must be operated on a twenty-four-hour basis. It is worth noting that because computers are often a major capital investment, managers are forced to keep the systems running the greater part of a twenty-four-hour day to recoup the cost. Up to the time of the introduction of computers, working in an office at night was rarely heard of; now there will be increased pressure for some people to give up the traditional 9 to 5 schedule to work on later shifts.

In several British studies dealing with computer changeover, researchers found that a computer engaged in office work is usually operated by a team consisting of three groups: programming staff—usually mathematicians and experts on methods study; operating group—comprising those who run the computer and auxiliary equipment; and maintenance technicians. Only a few people from the existing staff could be trained for the work, provided they had done well in algebra in school and were practical and creative.[20]

There is evidence that computers cause reorganization of the relationship between worker and supervisor. According to Mann, friendship patterns are broken up and there is a "loss of social anchorage."[21] Social relations tend to suffer as supervisors and subordinates are separated more by the pressure of work.

The worker is not the only one who submits to a computerized world. Even the middle-manager is being dramatically affected under the influence of electronic data processing. The computer has shown that many of the decisions traditionally made by management, and especially by middle-management, are routine and repetitive. As a result, business is finding less and less need for a middle-management unable to upgrade its skills. The American Foundation on Automation and Employment predicts a major change in what a manager of the future will be doing.[22] Many of his repetitive tasks will disappear and he will be faced with a greater variety of information requiring more rigorous analysis in decision-making. His span of control over his work and subordinates will be enlarged by the computer. His job will be more intellectually demanding and he will be rewarded with more freedom, more flexibility and more creativity in it. However, in order to remain a first-rate manager, he will be required to give more of himself than in the past. He will be constantly required to learn more on the job and to perceive relations between seemingly unrelated things. The future corporate manager, should he want to remain in the inner circle of executive decision-making, must accept the computer as an integral tool, must learn to utilize its potential, and must learn to submit to a host of new responsibilities that did not exist before its introduction.

"'Mind Stretching' for Management," was the title of a speech given by Dr. R. L. Martino, head of Olin Mathieson Chemical Corporation's Advanced Systems Department. He said, "A new brand of managers is urgently needed. The corporation executive of the 1970's will be seated behind a computer, not a desk . . . and the board room of the corporation of tomorrow will look like the war room of an army general with computers displaying all the pertinent information upon which the staff must make its decisions."[23]

Organizationally, each individual must accept the fact that in a computerized office he will have to lose part of his independence—accept the fact that he is merely a link in the total system. Few will be able to feel that they can thrive outside of the group. There will be greater centralization of social controls and decision-making. With the increased responsibilities, there will be reduction of autonomy in the human, who must serve as the connection in the machine process, and who tends to become more and more interdependent with other factors. Consequently, in choosing to work in computerized offices we may lose our importance as individuals to the importance of the team effort. From now on, there is going to be greater value placed on the operation as a whole. In other words, man is more and more an essential part of the system—but not as an individual, merely as one of its links.

Those who utilize the capabilities of the computer will have greater responsibility, ranging from determining the payroll checks of 5,000 employees in minutes, to evaluating test results for promotion and salary increases. In addition, the cost of the system and that of the personnel involved will weigh heavily on them. Responsibility is also greater because of the damage or loss that could result from their mistakes; individuals must be more conscientious and reliable. They must be "with it" at all times and will be reluctant to complain of headaches, hangovers or heartaches.

Thus, from the psychologist's point of view, there is an observable area of change in a computerized atmosphere. A number of the changes clearly result in added status, increased responsibility and attention, new skills and a different mix of skills. However, some assigned too-easy roles become bored; others assigned too-complex roles become fatigued. The fact that information can be processed in fractions of seconds with tremendous accuracy forces the rethinking and redesigning of the use of personnel. With greater integration of a work force, control is further centralized and the autonomy of branches reduced.

Simon Ramo illustrated how the student of the future would become more submissive to the computer. A system would register the student, giving him a small identification card along with his course plan. When he places this card into a computer, his complete record and present progress would be revealed. Although some time would be spent with people, according to Ramo, most of this student's school day would be consumed interacting with the computer.[24]

How the pupil submits to the computer while learning is another relatively unexplored issue. Educators have suggested that eventually the student will be housed in a room fitted with a complete retrieval system for data from any part of the world. Temperature controls will provide an unpolluted atmosphere to facilitate learning. By means of television, he will hear the lectures of outstanding instructors. The traditional teacher will now devote more of his time to the needs of the individual student.

Let us consider a situation that has been treated by several science fiction writers. Unable to escape, man will choose to allow the computer to dominate his being. A group of people (or nations) will evolve, linked together by the best of computer systems. Because of the apparently widening gap between the "haves" and "have-nots," the have-nots will have to be content with second-rate systems, and some people will have to accept the fact that, though free from the computer, they will be at a disadvantage with the possessors of computers. The result will be a struggle between those who resign themselves to the computer and turn wholeheartedly to it, and those who, in resisting the computer, are deprived of its power. This could result in a society composed of the rigid computer-users, who would have great difficulty adjusting to a dramatic environmental change; and those not as bound by the conditions of a formalized outlook, who could more appropriately find their way into a changing world. The outcome of this conflict could be staggering.

Another curious inroad that computers could make in our lives concerns the style of our everyday language. Today we communicate with computers by learning the electrically oriented machine language. With time the machine will know man's language. When the computer has learned to read, write, hear and speak man's language without error, even English might emerge as a standardized system. The computer will then become a very powerful force, imposing rigid restraints on language. A long-range effect might be that our language would become frozen, changing less frequently than it would under the influence of man's natural wishes.

Some experts believe that their computer systems can actually learn by themselves through trial and error. Analogous to the way children learn from their mistakes, this is referred to as the heuristic method. Nearly all computer researchers agree that the computer will eventually achieve close symbiosis with man, more and more informing and reforming his entire society. Thomas L. Whisler, Professor of Industrial Relations at the University of Chicago, appears to have predicted well in saying that the computer "will change everybody's life, and all change requires some effort and some cost to people."[25]

:

We have seen how the student and worker have been affected by the demands of the computer. Should one wish to become a member of the computer elite, he must submit himself further to an intensive program of evaluation and appraisal.

Submitting to a Screening Process

The key factor in whether the computer ultimately pays off is the "non-electronic brains"—the people who program and run the systems. Management is aware of the importance of sophisticated screening. Aside from the success or failure of the installation itself is the fact that some $10,000 may be invested in the training of a programmer. Therefore, to protect itself, the corporation submits individuals to an intensive examination process, beyond the basic "quickie" paper-and-pencil tests.

An appraisal of test aids currently available from manufacturers shows a spurt of interest in constructing or revising tests for programmers. Probably 6,000 programmers were employed in 1954 and the prospects are that 200,000 will be employed by 1970. The Programmers Aptitude Test (PAT) has long been used by International Business Machines. Like most instruments designed for computer personnel, this one consists of: (1) number series, which the examinee must complete after determining the pattern of the sequences given; (2) figure analogies, involving the recognition of the relationship between geometric figures; and (3) problems in arithmetic reasoning. As one psychologist puts it, "the test is good for rough screening—for skimming off the bottom." It was so widely used that it became "compromised" (psychologists' jargon for the fact that too many potential testees were already familiar with it), so the questions were altered in the 1959 version.

As a service to its computer customers, Radio Corporation

of America uses a battery of tests which cover numerical reasoning, verbal reasoning and abstract reasoning. These tests take up from one and a half to two hours, and can be administered by a customer, although grading and ranking are done by RCA itself. Those who rank in the bottom 25 per cent are rated as poor risks, those in the 26–74 per cent quartiles as somewhat questionable and those in the top quartile as those who potentially will do well.

Corporation users of computers can do some of their own screening. The computer customers of National Cash Register have an aptitude test for selecting potential computer programmers. The test takes about half an hour and consists of problems based on figures that are manipulated like data in a computer's memory, such as addition, looping, sequencing and comparing.

From these individual, packaged programs, consulting firms have developed tests in greater depth. The Diebold Personnel Selection Plan employs five basic tests in its battery: (1) The Symbols Block Diagram Test for programmers discovers whether a person can see how material can be logically arranged as a program. It is based on recognition of similarities in geometrical configurations. (2) The Code Index Test measures the ability to use a code index rapidly and accurately. It is a simple test for carelessness (disinterest) on highly routine chores. (3) The Relations in Numbers Test covers numerical series of the type already described. (4) The Code Matching Test measures the ability to make comparisons of coded material. It consists of a series of rather intricate exercises in substitutions of letters and numbers, which influence comparisons and selections. (5) The Word Sequence Test tests the ability to arrange words in order according to meaning, since the ability to deal with words and to arrange written reports are secondary abilities desired in programmers. Taking all five tests requires the better part of a day. Interpretations of test combinations are given for programmers, systems analysts and operators.

The Psychological Corporation uses tests as only one tool in the total process, relying also on close, in-depth work with employers in the screening of computer personnel, detailed information and analysis of job requirements, the applicants' potentials in terms of full utilization of talents, possibilities for promotion, and the like. Tests examine verbal ability, numerical ability, and abstract reasoning, but it is emphasized that these tests are not in the public domain, and are under close control (to guard against compromise). The Psychological Corporation has also developed an ingenious small, desk-top, electronic machine, called Logical Analysis Device (LAD), to test problem-solving ability, which all investigations have shown to be a highly important component in successful programming and systems analysis. Nine lights in a circular display panel can be turned on by adjacent push buttons. A target light in the center has no switch. The testee must find by experiment which combination of lights has the effect of turning on the center light. He is aided in planning his trials by an information diagram showing arrows linking pairs of lights. Each arrow represents one of three possible cause-effect relations. Analysis and experiment determine the effects of arrow relations that are not directly associated with the target light.

How accurate are these and other test batteries for measuring employee potential? Extremely little has been done to validate the tests for programmers (the same tests are used for systems analysts), comparing later performance on the job. The Psychological Corporation approached the Systems and Procedures Association with a plan for a comprehensive research project on analysts. There was initial enthusiasm, but the project was dropped because of the difficulty of establishing just what was to be tested. Apparently the only large-scale attempt at nailing down the predictive value of tests for programmers has been that of the Computer Personnel Research Group, sponsored by the U.S. Air Force under a RAND project. The report gives results of a test battery composed of IBM's PAT; TSI (Test of Sequential Instruction), especially constructed for the study; the Strong Vocational Interest Blank (400 items answered by "like-indifferent-dislike"); and a Personal Background Data Form, all administered to 534 programmers from the twenty-four participating companies. The sample was divided into two sub-samples:

301 scientific programmers and 233 business programmers. The data indicate that PAT and TSI correlated generally higher to the performance ratings by supervisors for the scientific sample than for the business sample. Some psychologists have contended that the problem of wide discrepancy between job performance and supervisors' ratings has not been overcome. There were some extremely high and some extremely low correlations for both PAT and TSI in individual organizations. The pattern that emerged from the Strong vocational interest test delineated a scientific, professionally-oriented, esthetic person. In addition, a number of specific items for this group are uniformly different from those of the general population—especially interest in mathematical subjects. These findings should contribute to the development of a separate key for programming as an occupation.

And still testing goes on, though its validity is limited. Also constantly under consideration are other approaches that would attempt to tell more about the aptitude and background of the individual in addition to what kind of personality he has. A person is submitted to careful screening if he wishes to enter this field. As the technology multiplies, it seems that we will have to pay for this efficiency by the partial loss of our identity, and changes in our personality. Are there no detours left along the road of psychological submission?

Resistance to new technologies is not unprecedented. "Sabotage" brings to mind an enemy agent planting a bomb. However, the word "sabotage" is derived from the French word *sabot*, wooden shoe. During the first industrial revolution, the production of clothing went from hand looms to mechanized looms. When these advanced looms were introduced into France in the late 1700s, some workers were afraid that they would lose their jobs. In an effort to protect themselves, they took their wooden shoes and threw them into the machine gears hoping to destroy the inevitable movement of industry and technology.

Norbert Wiener, shortly before his death, said: "The reprobation attaching in former ages to the sin of sorcery attaches now in many minds to the speculation of modern cybernetics. The future offers little hope for those who expect that our new mechanical slaves will offer us a world in which we may rest from thinking. Help us they may, but at the cost of supreme demands upon our honesty and our intelligence."[26]

An amusing skit appeared in the November, 1967, issue of *The Atlantic Monthly*, dramatizing how people would react under an operating federal data bank. In an entertaining way, it illustrates some very real possibilities. The entire play may be found in the Appendix.

CHAPTER VII

The People React

The deep alienation of man was aptly described in George Orwell's classic *1984*. Winston Smith struggles within himself to remain the controller of his own destiny. He resists submitting his total being to Big Brother. The battle over, Orwell concludes:

> He gazed up at the enormous face. Forty years it had taken him to learn what kind of smile was hidden beneath the dark mustache. O cruel, needless misunderstanding! O stubborn, self-willed exile from the loving breast! Two gin-scented tears trickled down the sides of his nose. But it was all right, everything was all right, the struggle was finished. He had won the victory over himself. He loved Big Brother.[1]

Winston Smith lost, but he fought to the end. There are some who believe that we have become so complacent and uncaring about our right to privacy that should this country become increasingly data-conscious, most citizens would sit by undisturbed. Has the American in the last third of the twentieth century become a mere automaton, no longer alert about the freedom so cherished by his ancestors? In that case, applied to today's conditions, was Justice Brandeis wrong when he said: "Men born to freedom are naturally alert to repel invasion of their liberty by evil minded rulers."[2]

People too often respond with indifference when they are not themselves directly affected by a problem. This is the case with wire tapping and electronic eavesdropping which touch only a few people in this country. Data collection and computerized data banks, however, will increasingly affect all of our lives, particularly if the information stored is vulnerable to misuse.

In an article, "1401 Is Watching," *Time* questioned how the public would react to data surveillance: "Today's Americans are a submissive lot. A generation ago, when someone suggested collecting everyone's fingerprints and filing them with the FBI, the civil libertarians shrieked with rage. But these days, hardly any U.S. auto driver knows—or seems to care—about a big grey machine in Washington. . . . It is a step toward a computerized Big Brotherhood that may one day be keeping elaborate tab on everybody."[3]

These words were echoed by Kahn and Wiener, "Because of the enormous importance of the national computer networks for planning and control . . . access to and control of the computers would become the focus of politics, conspiracy, and intraelite coups."[4]

The chairman of the House Subcommittee that investigated the computer and the invasion of privacy voiced this concern: "Through the standardization ushered in by technological advance, [man's] status in society would be measured by the computer, and he would lose his personal identity. His life, his talent, and his earning capacity would be reduced to a tape with very few alternatives available."[5] To date, experts all over the country have come to the aid of the general public in raising the many questions they feel should be asked before a national data bank is established and funded.

Probably the first major attempt to ascertain how the citizen feels about a data center was made in the spring of 1967. A graduate seminar* at Columbia University, headed by the author, attempted to categorize attitudes of various segments of the American population toward such an installation and also toward its possible ramifications. Three of the areas of discussion and concern to this research team were: (1) methods of collecting data; (2) use of data for federal government purposes, such as sociological research, combating discrimination in employment and aiding law enforcement agencies; and use of data for nongovernmental purposes, such as employment and promotion in private business and industry; and (3) extension of federal control and the possibilities of violation of Constitutional rights.

The study sought to discover citizens' attitudes about collection and use of data; relationship between the federal data bank and invasion of privacy; and increased federal control.

The final questionnaire contained eighteen items which could be answered in one out of the five following ways: (1) Agree Strongly; (2) Agree; (3) Neutral; (4) Disagree; or (5) Disagree Strongly. In addition, there were two open-ended questions, which required those tested to identify negative and positive effects that they believed would result from the collection of information in a centralized federal data bank.†

This questionnaire was distributed to 821 subjects; 510 by mail and 311 by direct contact. Of the mailed questionnaires, 129 were returned (25.3%). All questionnaires of those directly contacted were returned. The total sample of 440 included high school students, undergraduate college students, graduate students, deans of law schools, college teachers, college placement directors, personnel directors and corporation secretaries. (Questionnaires were distributed to all United States Senators, members of the United States Supreme Court and the fifty state labor organizations, but responses were so poor as not to permit meaningful interpretation for these groups.)

Obviously, this survey was far from definitive; nevertheless, the trends it appears to indicate may be telling.

* Participating students were: Robert Lundberg, Arlene Mahoney, Robert Miller, Dorothy Sharo, William Shipengrover and Stephen Zimney.
† See Appendix for questionnaire.

Before looking at the total population of 440 to determine the meaning and implications of their feelings, brief résumés of individual groups would be helpful. These are presented beginning with the group least negative toward the federal data bank, and ending with the group most negative.

Results from the High School Students

The sample of high school students came from a public system in a suburban New York City area; all were enrolled in a business course. Of the 89 students who completed the questionnaire, 79 indicated their sex (44 male and 35 female).

These high school students had both positive and negative opinions about the establishment of the data bank. They wanted to keep things private, and there was a marked concern that the individual who wanted to hide a past error would have a difficult time. Several of the teen-agers expressed fear of locating all this data in one place: "The loss of this data would be very bad." They were anxious that the entire center might be destroyed by fire, an explosion, sabotage or war.

Though fearful of more government control over the individual and over society as a whole, they did envision increased efficiency and the saving of time, money and space.

An unusual finding was that those individuals who were *not* aware of the federal data bank before this survey were more extreme in their attitudes than those who had known of the proposed system; one can infer that those who had heard of the bank were not so set in their views as those who had not. In other words, those who had heard of it had probably heard both negative and positive points and ultimately balanced the two out, while those who hadn't heard of the bank were influenced more by first impressions and their emotions.

Results from the Undergraduate College Students

This sample was taken from a four-year, public-supported institution in New York City. One hundred students completed the questionnaire. Of those who responded, all but one were under twenty-five. Fourteen of the respondents had heard about the federal data bank prior to the questionnaire, while sixty-six had not; twenty did not answer that question.

The most frequent concern of undergraduates seemed to be that a federal data bank would be an outright invasion of personal privacy. The possibility of gathering too much personal data about people was chilling; people want to be able to remain anonymous to some extent. The present dispersed systems give some assurance that all facts of one's life are not on display at one time; but a centralized system may not offer this safeguard. There was anxiety about information's getting into the wrong hands and a related threat of employee corruption.

Also, the "impersonality" of such a system was frequently voiced. The students seem to fear the realization of Huxley's *Brave New World* and the "Big Brother is watching you" society envisioned by Orwell in *1984*. Perhaps the impingement by government on too many personal activities is responsible for this feeling of loss of individuality. Or the speed and precision of the computer may be frightening to college students who have some experience with computerized installations which process grades, registration materials, and so forth.

The efficiency and economy of such a system seemed to make it worthwhile. Having information that is easily attainable at low' cost would be advantageous, if the suspicions about misuse of information could be discounted. Undergraduates seemed particularly positive about using such data to help law enforcement. However, favorable reaction to the use of data for discovering discriminatory practices in hiring and promoting workers was not as clear-cut.

Results from the Law Deans

The deans were selected from the *Law Teachers Directory* from different areas of the country. Eleven of the fifty questionnaires were returned: six from the South, three from the East, and two from the Central sections of the United States. All of the deans were male and all but one were above thirty-six years of age. Seven had heard of the federal data bank, three had not and one did not respond to the question.

They saw the bank as a worthwhile investment for purposes of efficiency in bookkeeping and clerking, assisting in law enforcement, uniformity and cutting down on the need to fill out questionnaires. However, they envisioned "creation of a 'sterile elite,' i.e., those about whom no negative information is on record," and "automatic reliance upon data."

They were most opposed to data from such a bank's being available to private industry, reflecting the lawyer's concern with violation of the individual's rights in obtaining employment. The information might allow employers to discriminate very readily against certain kinds of people, e.g., those with arrest records. The deans' responses to items on hiring, promotion, and discrimination bear this out. As one would expect, they were also very concerned about the loss of the individual's Constitutional rights.

Results from the College Professors

One hundred and fifty questionnaires were sent to professors listed at Wisconsin State University. This university was selected in the belief that it was a typical, large, Midwestern, "voice of America," institution of higher learning. Sixty questionnaires were returned (40 per cent). Thirty-two per cent were in the age group from 25 to 35 years, 36 per cent in the age group from 36 to 50 years; and 32 per cent were above 50. Five did not give their ages. Of those who responded, 7 were female and 50 male.

As might be expected, many felt that the proposed federal data bank would increase efficiency in the federal government. The Wisconsin professors indicated that they felt the bank would threaten privacy by exerting more control over the individual. "This carried to its logical conclusion would mean the harnessing of human thought, incentives, judgments, opportunities, and development of a closed society." They strongly felt that the individual should be allowed to review his personal data and that release of information from a federal data bank should have the approval of the individual concerned lest there be "further loss of individual rights to privacy, labelling of an individual particularly for unwise or unfortunate acts in youth. The individual in our society must have the opportunity to become what he will, rather than what he has been." A centralized data bank might force individuals to hide their activities.

Most of the professors felt that information would not be an aid to undesirable elements of our society such as the underworld. They did, however, express the opinion that data should not be released to private industry: "Should all our mistakes follow us throughout life?"

Results from College Placement Directors

The group of college placement directors was solicited completely by mail. A response of 40 out of 118 was obtained. The group was chosen from the *College Placement Annual*, with an emphasis placed on at least two select schools from each of the fifty states. Nine forms from the East and the same number from the South were counted, as well as ten and twelve from the West and Central respectively. Most of the group were over thirty-five years of age and most were males. In addition, 26 out of 36 reported having had prior knowledge of the federal data bank. (Four did not respond.)

The overall attitude of the group tended toward the negative, especially on questions dealing with privacy and government controls. It is interesting to note that, despite their concern, the placement-director group failed to agree with an item that warned of the possible aid of the bank to criminal elements of this society. This could be attributed to their apparent naïvety regarding that type of corruption.

In addition, on the question dealing with the basic concept of civil liberties, the group did not show consistent attitudes regarding the sanctity of certain kinds of personal information. It appears that philosophical items dealing with Constitutionality elicit differences of opinion within this group despite their general agreement on specific, well-defined Constitutional rights.

Results from the Graduate Students

The sample was taken from a hundred graduate students at a university in New York City. Though they came from various parts of the country, the students listed themselves under the East because of the location of the school. There were 49 males and 49 females (two failed to respond to this item). Fifty-six were below 25 years of age; 31 between 25 and 35 years; 8 between 36 and 50 (five did not respond). Thirty-seven of the students had heard of the federal data bank, 41 had not and 22 did not answer this question.

These students seemed most concerned about loss of individualism, lack of privacy, control over the individual and misuse of information. Some saw the bank as centralized power, which would be recklessly used in exploiting the individual and blackmailing society.

On the positive side, they saw the bank as one of the most efficient operations ever to be developed—able to answer requests for information quickly and accurately. It was seen as an instrument that would provide a wealth of economic advice on consumer prediction, social research and communications.

This concern for efficiency could be attributed to the fact that graduate students may be the greatest users of such a bank in their independent and graduate research projects.

They clearly want a voice in determining what information will go into the bank and who will be permitted to see it. Of all the sample groups, this one would probably be the most activist and questioning if such a bank were officially developed. They are vocal on issues; they have the necessary annoyance with such a project; and they are concerned about whether the bank would affect their future property, employment, family and status.

The chances are that had more of the students heard of the bank, and had they been aware of its wide range of capabilities, they would have been even more negative in their attitudes toward it.

Results from the Industrial Personnel Directors

Eighteen personnel directors responded, out of a total mail solicitation of a hundred. The employers of the eighteen respondents were all among the hundred largest U.S. corporations, as listed in the July, 1966, *Fortune*. Three directors were between the ages of 25 and 35; seven were between the ages of 36 and 50; four were more than 50 years of age; and four did not respond to this item. Eight were from the Eastern region of the country, two from the South, six from the Central region and two from the Western coast. Only two of the respondents had less than a college degree. Ten of the personnel directors had previously heard of the federal data bank, five had not and three failed to answer the question.

While the personnel directors tended to feel strongly that individual privacy would be threatened by a federal data bank, they were in even greater agreement in their general distrust of how the data would be used. Thus, they emphatically held that there should be limitations on the kinds of information to be included in the data bank; that release of data should be limited to the purposes intended; that private industry should not have access to the data bank; and that individuals should have the right to review and disagree with the information included. They also tended to agree that the data would not assist either in increasing the accuracy of employment decisions or in locating discrimination in employment.

The personnel directors thus seemed to be objecting to the federal data bank primarily because of specific problems they envisioned in its administration and control. As they all worked for very large organizations, it is probable that the respondents had encountered both computerized data centers and inept bureaucratic administration. Either due to this exposure or to their general experience in the business world, the sample of personnel directors focused on the specific operating problems of a federal data bank rather than the more general issue of invasion of privacy. The prime negative outcome of a federal data bank, to these people, would be either increased bureaucratic control or possible misuse of data.

Results from the Industrial Secretaries

Twenty-two secretaries working in the East Coast headquarters of an industrial firm with approximately 9,000 employees were asked to complete the questionnaire. Ten respondents were less than 25 years of age, nine were between 25 and 35 and three failed to give their ages. One respondent had a college degree, twelve had at least a high school diploma, and nine did not respond to this question. Three had previously heard of the federal data bank, fifteen had not, and four did not answer this item.

It is of interest to note that the issue about which the secretarial group felt most strongly was whether the data from the federal data bank should be made available to private industry. Only one secretary felt that private industry should have access to the data bank, while twenty disagreed. (One failed to answer.) This seems to be not so much an expression of distrust of private industry, as a rejection of a specific procedure that would threaten their individual privacy. (In fact it would be surprising to find a group outside of the private sector that would perceive this issue as personally threatening in this way.)

The remaining strongly felt responses all dealt with the desire of the individual to maintain some control over his own destiny. The secretarial group did not want to yield this responsibility to an impersonal centralized data center. They strongly held that a federal data bank could be a threat to individual privacy and rights, that release of data requires permission of the individual concerned, and that increased federal control would result from use of such a bank. While some potential benefits were seen by fifteen of the secretaries, twenty of the twenty-two sampled expressed great concern that data could be improperly used and that individual privacy and Constitutional rights would be greatly endangered by such a centralized federal computer-facility.

Results of the Total Sample Population

While earlier sections dealt with the manner in which specific groups responded to the questionnaire, this total summary emphasizes intergroup differences and touches upon the effects of demographic and background variables upon attitudes toward the federal data bank.

The range of scores was from 5.0, indicating the most negative attitude, to 1.0, indicating the most positive attitude toward the proposed data facility. The relative strength of attitudes toward the federal data bank was distributed in the following manner from the items in the questionnaire:

High School Students	2.65
College Students	2.82
Law Deans	3.07
Professors	3.10
Placement Directors	3.20
Graduate Students	3.21
Personnel Directors	3.23
Company Secretaries	3.28

The following are the major results, presented in descending rank order (strongest response first):

1. A federal data bank can be a threat to Constitutional rights.
2. An individual should be allowed to review and disagree with any information stored on him in a federal data bank.
3. Release of data should be limited to the purpose for which it was intended.
4. Information about individuals should not be made available to private industry.

From the background and demographic data, the following appeared:

1. Virtually no statistical differences were found in attitude on the basis of sex.
2. There was an indication that, as contrasted with the younger population, respondents over the age of thirty-five tend to hold more negative attitudes.
3. While significant differences existed between the attitudes of the population sampled in the Western region of the country and other regions, no strong trend was indicated here, because of the limited size of the Western sample. In any case, those in the Central and Southern regions appeared to possess attitudes more positive than those in the coastal regions of the country.
4. Educational differences seemed to contribute to some

of the variability between groups; those individuals possessing at least a college degree are more negatively disposed to the federal data bank than the remainder of the population. (The exception was the corporate secretaries.)

5. Respondents employed by private industry are consistently more negative toward the federal data bank than those employed by non-profit institutions or those not employed (usually students).

6. Those who had previous knowledge of the data-collecting facility possess more negative attitudes toward it.

Some Conclusions

The most significant conclusion derived from this survey was that an important relationship exists between negative attitudes toward the federal data bank and the degree of exposure to computerized data-gathering facilities.

For instance, looking at the total group averages, it was interesting to note that even though high school students and secretaries have relatively similar educational backgrounds, they exhibit, respectively, the most favorable and least favorable attitudes toward the concept of the federal data bank. It appears reasonable to assume that the differences are primarily due to the fact that the secretarial group knew something about the use of computers in industry. This assumption is supported by the unfavorable attitudes of the personnel director and graduate student groups, both of which surely have had some exposure to computerized data-gathering facilities.

In examining the background and demographic data which would seem to relate most highly with opportunity for awareness of computerization, i.e., age, education, and employer, this was corroborated.

:

Privacy is the right of the individual to decide for himself how much of his life—his thoughts, emotions and the facts that are personal to him—he will share with others.

What is most disturbing to the American population is the

undemocratic process which starts at birth to make people believe that they are unable to say *no* to divulging personal information, thus perpetuating a collection of data that will follow them for the remainder of their lives—"frozen in time and the computer."

People want to determine for themselves in every particular situation of life just how much of their complex beliefs, attitudes and actions they choose to disclose. To the American, this data is more than just statistics. It is the data of judgment, a possible last judgment that can affect their schooling, employment possibilities, promotion, or role in the community. The citizens of this country want to have the right to a personal diary that is away and free from the government's outstretched hands. They plead the case that if all their actions were documented, including their mistakes, it would be difficult to close a page of one's life and start anew.

Raymond Katzell, Chairman of the Psychology Department at New York University, has spoken about protecting privacy. Confining men in close quarters physically and socially, as in submarines, he points out, would make them particularly prone to peevishness and mutual hostility. Employing the phrases "getting away" and "letting go," Katzell suggests that vacationers are really seeking to avoid the pervasive inspection by society. "In short, there is reason to believe that a modicum of privacy is a necessary condition to mental and emotional well-being. Conceivably, a society which fails sufficiently to preserve the individual's privacy may become characterized by undesirable behavior patterns such as irritability, mistrust, and hostility."[6]

Recently, Richard S. Barrett conducted a survey, within the Division of Industrial Psychology of the American Psychological Association, on attitudes toward invasion of privacy.[7] Four hundred and seventy-five questionnaires were returned. In an attempt to determine psychologists' attitudes toward collecting specific types of data for purposes of employment, the following percentages were determined (see facing page).

We have seen that, when directly confronted with the issue of the federal data bank, people do indeed react. High school and college students, professors and psychologists—all emerge with some surprisingly strong attitudes. And the awareness

	Acceptable in almost every respect	Generally acceptable, some questionable features	Not acceptable because of invasion of privacy	No opinion	Depends	No response
Previous earnings	67	22	5	1	1	4
Financial assets and liabilities	25	37	30	2	2	4
Relations with parents and siblings	17	40	35	2	2	4
Marital adjustment	15	40	36	1	3	5
Sexual deviation	11	23	54	4	3	5
Age	77	15	2	1	1	4
Racial or ethnic background	25	33	36	2	1	3
Religious beliefs	10	20	63	2	2	3
Political beliefs	9	19	66	2	1	3
School grades	75	18	2	1	1	3
Extra curricular activities	75	17	2	1	1	4
Address and telephone number	91	3	1	1	1	3
Tested intelligence	66	25	3	1	1	4
General health	80	15	0	0	1	4
Digestion, "nervous stomach"	43	39	10	2	1	5
Use of alcohol	38	43	12	1	1	5
Use of habit-forming drugs	44	35	14	1	1	5
Police record	44	36	13	2	2	3
Psychiatric history	23	38	31	2	3	3

should grow. System Development Corporation Vice-President Dr. Thomas Rowan has said: "Clearly there should be an awareness of the potential hazards of an omnipotent government information system and a sensitivity to establishing safeguards against the invasion of individual privacy. . . . Public distress about the specter of an omniscient Big Brother goverment seems to be growing."[8]

The snowballing effect becomes very real. The more you know, the more you want to know and the better your methods will become to get this information. In the end, will there be any place to hide?

The quest for privacy is a strong one. The poet Robert Browning said in "Paracelsus":

I give the fight up: let there be an end,
A privacy, an obscure nook for me.
I want to be forgotten even by God.[9]

CHAPTER VIII

Protecting Our Constitutional Rights

Pope Pius XII once observed: "And just as it is illicit to appropriate another's goods or to make an attempt on his bodily integrity, without his consent, so it is not permissible to enter into his inner domain against his will, whatever is the technique or method used."[1]

We are slowly drifting into a world of nakedness. Each year an increasing number of technological devices invade the world that we once considered private and personal. In spite of this, we are still confident that our lives, activities, ideas, thoughts, and sensations are shared with no one unless we so chose.

Traditionally this cherished belief has been based on a confidence that the federal government would set the pattern that the rest of the nation would follow. In fact, two or three decades from now, unless the government intervenes, there will be few questions left to ask about privacy; we will have taken for granted a society in which everything about us may be revealed.

It will be difficult to protest unguarded data surveillance if the federal government fails to set itself up as a safety model against information leakage. In addition to protecting the security of the nation, the government must be responsible for protection of individual rights. FBI Director J. Edgar Hoover stated: "We must demonstrate that the freedoms Americans cherish so highly are strengthened whenever law enforcement asserts itself not only in crime and subversion but also against any invasion upon the rights and dignity of all the people."[2] It must not be possible for the government to use amassed information for coercion or exposure which violates due process. For example, the rules governing the Bureau of the Census are intended to assure us that information released to it will never be used against us for purposes of Congressional investigation or tax enforcement.

Despite past protections, proposed data banks would create a new environment that would require different evaluations of our rights to protection. Under Secretary of Defense Walter J. Skallerup, Jr., warned: "Inquiries which have no relevance to a security determination should not be made. Questions regarding personal and domestic affairs, financial matters, and the status of physical health fall in this category unless evidence clearly indicates a reasonable basis for believing there may be illegal or subversive activities, personal or immoral irresponsibility, or mental or emotional instability involved. The probing of a person's thoughts and beliefs and questions about his conduct, which have no security implications, are unwarranted."[3]

A major problem in protecting our privacy is that too often we believe in the principle that the ends justify the means. When we consider that the goal is the greater good of our people, we cannot understand why a specific intrusion should be prohibited. The result: gradual erosion of the value we place on individual privacy. Sometimes we are confused and become easily convinced that a particular device that may lead to personal intrusion is warranted on other grounds, such as purposes of security. This is an inadequate argument.

Information has been exchanged between departments for decades. The Justice Department, FBI, Immigration and Naturalization Service, Secret Service, Bureau of Customs, Internal

Revenue Service, and the Federal Bureau of Narcotics, among others, share much of their information from central files. This results in a more efficient fight against crime and other matters affecting security.

In addition to the Internal Revenue Service, other agencies have the right to examine an individual's tax return. In 1963, nine Congressional committees were entitled to call for any tax return filed by a U.S. taxpayer for the preceding several years, and some for any year since 1947. Also the House Ways and Means Committee, the Senate Finance Committee and the Joint Congressional Committee on Internal Revenue Taxation, which are responsible for legislation involving taxation, have the right, by law, to inspect returns.

Vance Packard reveals that individual tax returns or excerpts have been used by the Department of Defense. Some years ago, Barry Goldwater, then Senator from Arizona, charged on the Senate floor that the Deputy Assistant Secretary of Defense for Civil Rights had been using "the full force" of income tax returns to coerce local businessmen into desegregating business establishments near military bases.[4]

Another powerful reservoir of information is the National Agency Check conducted by investigators within the Defense Department. Checks are made on individuals who are being considered for employment that gives them access to defense information. In one year alone nearly 700,000 individuals were reviewed and files made on them. The National Agency Check has access to FBI criminal and subversive files, intelligence files, military files, Civil Service Commission files (where applicable), immigration files (where applicable), and House Un-American Activities Committee files (where applicable).

Information given to the government is on a confidential basis and for a specific purpose. Two issues are at stake: whether the information is relevant when employed for purposes other than the original one, and whether there is a threat to Constitutional rights.

Stored information becomes less and less relevant and more and more misleading over a period of years.

It would rarely be the case that an exhaustive record on an individual would be considered essential to the public good. The exceptions might be those whose actions affect others directly. For example, if we had more data on and therefore more understanding about bus drivers, airline pilots and train conductors, we might be able to improve methods of selection and training. However, the number of people whose employment relates directly to life-and-death situations is quite small.

Professor Charles Reich of the Yale Law School, in discussing the secrecy involved in a data bank, emphasizes, ". . . this is a denial of the Constitutional right to confront, the Constitutional right to face those who make statements about you, to question them, and to rebut, to answer." One does not have to be accused of a crime to find himself seriously harmed by the disclosed data. The criminal is entitled to a trial and a lawyer. The "notion of petrification," says Reich, exists when a man is accused, and as a result is labeled bad forever. There is no present defense against this.[5]

One could protest the manner in which government files are filled with information about individuals. According to John J. Pemberton, Jr., Executive Director of the American Civil Liberties Union: "Unfortunately, the great bulk of information about an individual is not gathered as the result of inquiries by skilled Government security investigators. Rather, it is often acquired by Government employees of poor judgment, by private agencies, credit unions, insurance companies and businesses."[6] The various agencies of the government farm out investigative work to a host of private firms. Once the gathered information is recorded on a file, the chances are that it will remain on permanent record.

The concern to limit government intrusion on the individual's behavior dates back far beyond American history. In 430 B.C. Pericles warned the Athenians:

> The freedom we enjoy in our Government extends also to our private life. There, far from exercising a jealous surveillance over each other, we do not feel called upon to be angry with our neighbor for doing what he likes, or even to indulge in those injurious looks which cannot fail to be offensive, although they inflict no positive penalty. But all this ease in our private relations does not make us lawless as citizens. Against this fear is our chief safeguard, teaching us to obey the magistrates and the laws,

particularly such as regard the protection of the injured, whether they are actually on the statute book or belong to that code which, although written, yet cannot be broken without acknowledged disgrace.[7]

Our rights as Americans were not easily come by. Shortly after the Constitution was adopted, James Madison proposed the addition of twelve amendments. Thomas Jefferson wrote to Madison: "A Bill of Rights is what the people are entitled to against every government on earth, general or particular; and what no just government should refuse or rest on inference."

He wanted words "providing clearly, and without the aid of sophism, for freedom of religion, freedom of the press, protection against standing armies, restriction of monopolies, the eternal and unremitting force of the habeas corpus laws, and trials by jury in all matters of fact triable by the laws of the land, and not by the laws of nations."

Alexander Hamilton, however, felt that the Constitution already covered these rights adequately: "I go further, and affirm that bills of rights, in the sense and to the extent in which they are contended for, are not only unnecessary . . . but would even be dangerous. They would contain various exceptions to powers not granted; and, on this very account, would afford a colorable pretext to claim more than were granted. . . . The truth is . . . that the Constitution is itself, in every rational sense, and to every rational purpose, a bill of rights."

But Jefferson was concerned about the fact that those who were responsible for the development of the Constitution would not be around forever, and that the leaders who would follow might be less enthusiastic about rights to freedom and liberty. He was afraid that, once the country's security was assumed to be guaranteed, people's attentions would gradually shift from concern for national survival to individual financial success. "They will forget themselves, but in the sole faculty of making money, and will never think of uniting to effect a due respect for their rights."[8] Jefferson and Madison were victorious.*

* See Appendix for complete Bill of Rights.

Thus our tradition of privacy has its protective roots in provisions of the Constitution and the Bill of Rights: Free speech, expression and belief; religious freedom and free conscience; protection against search without proper warrant and for unreasonable demands; protection from force to incriminate oneself; and protection from cruel and unusual punishment.

Invasion of privacy was not much of a threat in the nontechnological eighteenth century. At the time the Constitution was written, all communication was by speech or letter, and the only form of surveillance was watching or listening. Few records were kept on the general population. There were laws to protect the privacy of home, person and the process of communication, and provisions to protect against self-incrimination and government coercion to elicit information. The major protections against invasion of personality were written into the First Amendment, which guaranteed free speech, press, assembly, and religion.

Commencing with the early nineteenth century, there were several court decisions that helped to define Constitutional rights. "Private sentiment" and "private judgment" came to be accepted as rights following the decision by Justice Joseph Story in 1833.[9] In 1853 Francis Lieber, a leading authority on public law, said that the first amendment was intended to protect "freedom of communion," including "liberty of silence," the right not to have to speak, and "the sacredness of epistolary communion."[10] He was underlining the right of an individual to have relationships with others that would not be interrupted or submitted to surveillance by those in public or private power. We must have freedom to associate without unreasonable surveillance, said Lieber, from "the spy, the mouchard, the dilator, the informer, and the sycophant" of a police government.[12]

According to James Holbrook, writing in 1855:

> The laws of the land are intended not only to preserve the person and material property of every citizen sacred from intrusion, but to secure the privacy of his thoughts, so far as he sees fit to withhold them from others. Silence is as great a privilege as speech, and it is as important that every one should be able to maintain it whenever he

pleases, as that he should be at liberty to utter his thoughts without restraint.[11]

In 1825 the federal mail statute forbade anyone to open any letter "to pry into another's business or secret." The case of Denis v. Leclerc, decided in 1811, held that the holder of a letter did not have the right to publish it without the consent of the writer. In a case in 1831, a Pennsylvania judge proclaimed: "Everyman's house is his castle, where no man has a right to intrude for any purpose whatever. No man has a right to pry into your secrecy in your own house. There are very few families where even the truth would not be very unpleasant to be told all over the country."[13]

After the Civil War, technological innovations made possible violations of privacy. With the telephone, a private conversation relayed across wires could be overheard. The microphone in the seventies and the dictograph in the nineties made it possible to record conversations without detection. With the development of photography, a visual record of one's state or behavior could be made and kept.

According to Professor Alan Westin, author of *Privacy and Freedom*, "American laws failed to come to grips with these new challenges in the years between 1880 and 1950."[14] Between 1890 and 1950, only 2 of the 300 reported cases involving the common-law right of privacy were actions for damages against private parties for using surveillance devices, and there were no recoveries against government intrusions, even when the police acted without authority or for illegal purposes such as extortion.

Samuel D. Warren, a law partner of Louis D. Brandeis, married a prominent society lady in 1883 and proceeded to give a whirl of parties in his Boston home. One of the local newspapers reported many of these events in a rather sensational fashion. Annoyed, he and Brandeis wrote an article, "The Right of Privacy," which appeared in the December 15, 1890, issue of the *Harvard Law Review*. They said:

> The Press is overstepping in every direction the obvious bounds of propriety and decency. Gossip is no longer the recourse of the idle and the vicious, but has become a

trade, which is pursued with industry as well as effrontery. To satisfy a prurient taste the details of sexual relations are spread broadcast in the columns of the daily papers. To occupy the indolent, column upon column is filled with idle gossip, which can only be procured by invasion upon the domestic circle.[15]

The fourth amendment was challenged in 1928 in Olmstead v. United States. Olmstead and fifty other persons were charged with being part of a bootleg ring operating out of Seattle, Washington. Over a five-month period, evidence was gathered against the group by means of wiretaps placed on eight telephones. The government printed 775 typewritten pages of notes on the conversations overheard. The issue at hand was whether the fourth amendment made wiretapping unconstitutional. The answer, by a margin vote of one, was that it did not. Writing for the majority, Chief Justice William Howard Taft held: "The Amendment does not forbid what was done here. There was no searching. There was no seizure. The evidence was secured by the use of the sense of hearing and that only. There was no entry of the houses or offices of the defendants."[16]

In his famous dissent, Judge Brandeis replied:

> The makers of our Constitution undertook to secure conditions favorable to the pursuit of happiness. They recognized the significance of man's spiritual nature, of his feelings and of his intellect. . . . They conferred, as against the Government, the right to be let alone—the most comprehensive of rights and the right most valued by civilized man. To protect that right, every unjustifiable intrusion by the Government upon the privacy of the individual, whatever the means employed, must be deemed a violation of the fourth amendment.[17]

Justice Oliver Wendell Holmes, dissenting in the same case, made an equally strong point about government's role in criminal detection:

> It is desirable that criminals should be detected, and to that end all available evidence should be used. It is also

desirable that the Government should not itself foster and pay for other crimes, when they are the means by which the evidence is to be obtained. . . . We have to choose, and for my part, I think it a less evil that some criminals should escape than that the Government play an ignoble part.[18]

By and large, the Supreme Court's decisions in the area of invasion of privacy were until very recently weak and ineffective. What was lacking was a general Constitutional interpretation of what was meant by privacy. The Supreme Court failed to find in the first amendment a strong basis for the right to privacy. "Privacy," according to Westin, "was thus a passive virtue that was invoked only to place *limits* on assertions of freedom of speech."[19]

There are four states of privacy that may be threatened in the future.[20] When a person is separated from his group and freed from observation by others, this state of privacy is called *solitude*. Although he continues to be subject to nature—rain, smog, air pollution; to his physical conditions—coughs, itching and feelings of pain; to the influence of his thoughts, soul or conscience—this is the most complete state of aloneness a person can reach. Does the use of information retrieved from a data bank invade one's right to *solitude*?

The choice to select one's friend or mate is part of the second state of privacy known as *intimacy*. He should possess the freedom to select those persons that he wishes to take into his confidence and be secure in knowing that he is free to say what is on his mind without the threat of surveillance. Does the use of information retrieved from a data bank invade *intimacy*?

When in a public place, riding a subway, walking through a museum or park, the ability to remain free from identification and surveillance is the state of privacy known as *anonymity*. Constant observation or fear of observation in public tends to destroy the feeling of security and freedom that we all expect. Anonymity makes it possible to start a conversation with a stranger and not be concerned that the information will be affixed to our record. Does the use of information retrieved from a data bank invade *anonymity*?

Lastly, the choice to hold back information about ourselves is *reserve*. No one should be forced to tell more about himself than he chooses, no one should be forced to communicate a part of his life's experience if he chooses not to do so. Does the use of information retrieved from a data bank infringe on *reserve*?

In our society we believe in the uniqueness of each person, his basic worth as an individual. To this end we approve of "personal autonomy" as a prime function of privacy. We have committed ourselves in the past to upholding the belief that under normal circumstances no one should be permitted to pry into an individual's personal life. Since in many respects each of us lives behind a mask, we should also possess the right to keep the personality behind the mask out of a file repository.

In *The Pattern of Liberty*, Clinton Rossiter has emphasized this point:

> Privacy is a special kind of independence, which can be understood as an attempt to secure autonomy in at least a few personal and spiritual concerns, if necessary in defiance of all the pressures of modern society . . . [I]t seeks to erect an unreachable wall of dignity and reserve against the entire world. The free man is the private man, the man who still keeps some of his thoughts and judgments entirely to himself, who feels no over-riding compulsion to share everything of value with others, not even with those he loves and trusts.[21]

Emotional release is a function of privacy. We should be permitted to occasionally escape the pressures of our social role. We should be permitted occasionally to "let off steam," to be angry, to cry out our emotions without fear of interference or criticism. And certainly, during moments of stress, a death in our family, illness, we should be allowed periods of emotional release to behave as we feel, as long as this does no harm to another.

Time and privacy must be set aside for each of us to evaluate and reevaluate the "why" of life; we must be given the sanctuary of freedom to contemplate our being and future.

We must be allowed periods for looking at past events and for internal communication to find the means to continue living with ourselves. We must also be given the chance to decide to whom we will entrust our thoughts, and to whom we will reveal our secrets; and to determine what types of associations we wish to develop.

We must possess a "limited and protected communication." We must be allowed to develop and to hold a psychological distance from others in respect to the quantity and quality of what we reveal—to be naked before another in conversation is to throw away our remaining defenses.

Can anyone deny the tragedy that would result if accounts were kept of our emotional outbursts, our choices to isolate ourselves for periods of contemplation, and which of our friends were most knowledgeable about our thoughts and activities.

In addition, according to Westin, "Privacy performs the same basic functions for organizations, governmental and private, that it does for individuals; it contributes to the achievement of organizational autonomy, releases the organization members from formal role compliance, provides internal evaluation to prepare organizational policies, and protects the organization's limited communication with others."[22]

As the technology of the late nineteenth century began to take hold, the legal and judicial minds of the country searched for Constitutional protections against privacy invasion. The issue at hand was whether a nation that was emerging technologically could remain free if the pattern continued to develop whereby the invention, not the man, became central.

The fourth amendment in the Bill of Rights was of little value in the interpretation of Constitutional invasion of personal rights. In the Brown v. Walker case in 1896 the Supreme Court decided that the privilege could be claimed only when a witness feared persecution, not when he wished to protect reputation or private affairs from compulsory exposure and community disapproval.

Consequently, based on the then current interpretation of the Constitution and the Bill of Rights, the individual had little guarantee that, with further sophistication in data surveillance of his personal life, he would survive the conflict between anonymity and technology. In part because of the lack of corrective interpretations in this area, the courts throughout the nation were hard pressed to salvage this freedom after the end of the Second World War. In addition, the increasing use of the fifth amendment to refuse to incriminate oneself worried some lawmakers and interpreters of law.

Since it is naive to think that all data surveillance can be eliminated, specific criteria must be evolved. Westin makes the following suggestions: "Police want to solve crimes, corporations to control thefts, employers to select more successful employees, news media to tell the 'inside' story about leading persons and events, educators to identify personality problems in school children, behavioral scientists to observe real-life situations. But if all that need be done to win legal and social approval for surveillance is to indicate a social need and show that surveillance would help cope with it, there is no balancing at all, only a qualifying procedure to license to invade privacy. Therefore, the need involved must be serious enough to overcome the very real risk of jeopardizing the public's confidence in its daily freedom from unreasonable invasions of privacy."[23]

There are often several methods available to accomplish a given social end. The burden of proof should be on those who seek authorization for surveillance to show that there are not alternative techniques available which do less violence to individual and organizational privacy.

The degree of reliability of the surveillance instrument must also be taken into account.

The problem of consent to invasion of privacy is a complicated one. Is an individual's consent implied by the fact that he accepts a certain kind of job, or that he has permitted certain kinds of surveillance previously? School teachers, for example, are accustomed to having their classrooms visited by principals; does their consent to this long-standing practice imply consent to the use of loudspeaker boxes by which administrators can monitor a classroom without the knowledge of teacher or pupils?

In the past twenty years the courts have been able to slowly evolve an operational definition of Constitutional privacy. The

Supreme Court responded to technological surveillance as follows:

> The Court has indicated the need for emotional release and self-evaluation by individuals in its decisions on privacy from raucous sound trucks and in the cases protecting the privacy of householders from aggressive solicitors;
>
> The Court has protected the permissible deviation function of privacy by guarding the privacy of children who do not want to salute the flag or recite prayers in school because of their religious beliefs, as well as the privacy of university professors in their classroom and campus expressions;
>
> The Court has recognized the intimacy function with its ruling guaranteeing marital privacy;
>
> The Court has recognized individual and group needs for anonymity and preparatory privacy by its rulings on privacy of associations' membership rolls, anonymity in individual political publications, and the concept of "breathing space" for the exercise of first amendment rights;
>
> The Court has protected privacy's function as a protector of modesty with decisions on the inviolability of the body from stomach pumping and other unreasonable physical inspections or intrusions;
>
> The Court has extended some protection to the confessional function of privacy in decisions on the right to privacy from government surveillance in the lawyer-client relationship.[24]

Probably the most outspoken leader in the fight to protect privacy in the Supreme Court is Justice William Joseph Brennan. Referring to the 1963 Lopez v. United States case, he wrote:

> Electronic surveillance strikes deeper than the ancient feeling that man's home is his castle; it strikes at freedom

of communication, a postulate of our kind of society. . . . Freedom of speech is undermined where people fear to speak unconstrainedly in what they suppose to be the privacy of home and office.

Continuing, he emphasized the right to anonymity and associational privacy:

The right of privacy is the obverse of freedom of speech in another sense. This Court has lately recognized that the First Amendment freedoms may include the right, under certain circumstances, to anonymity. . . . Electronic surveillance destroys all anonymity and privacy . . . it makes government privy to everything that goes on.[25]

This is not to say that laws and regulations do not exist to protect against loose distribution of data on individuals. There are numerous protections which in the past have usually been adequate. For instance, under penalty of the law, information given to the federal government for statistical purposes is not to be released in any form whereby any particular individual or business establishment can be identified. When this confidentiality has not been adhered to, the courts have responded. The Supreme Court, in St. Regis Paper Co. v. United States, stated that the confidentiality provisions of the census law prohibited the subpoena of an organization's own copy of its census return. The Administration supported this viewpoint and Congress appropriately passed corrective legislation to give to the copy the same confidentiality and immunity from legal process as due the original.

The Federal Reports Act of 1942, section 4(a),[26] provides that in the event that information obtained in confidence by a federal agency is released to another agency, all the provisions of law relating to protection of the information from unlawful disclosure by the collecting agency are also applicable to the agency to which the information is released. This includes penalties.

Title 18, United States Code, Section 1905, provides for penalties (fine or imprisonment, or both, and removal from office) for federal employees found tampering with confidential statistical data.[27] Section 139 (b) of Title V of the United States Code reads:

> Information obtained by a Federal agency from any person or persons may pursuant to section 139–139f of this title, be released to any other Federal agency only if (1) the information shall be released in the form of statistical totals or summaries; or (2) the information as supplied by persons to a Federal agency shall not, at the time of collection, have been declared by that agency or by any superior authority to be confidential; or (3) the persons supplying the information shall consent to the release of it to a second agency by the agency to which the information was originally supplied; or (4) the Federal agency to which another Federal agency shall release the information has authority to collect the information itself and such authority is supported by legal provisions for criminal penalties against persons failing to supply such information.[28]

Although penalties exist to protect both individuals and businesses, it remains an open issue how these protections would be employed in a federal data center or series of data banks. It is doubtful that the present laws are adequate in light of the changing capabilities and exposures presented by the computer. Stretching the interpretation of present laws and regulations may only prove to be a greater frustration than the writing of new provisions.

New York State, in order to raise some extra revenue, sold the names and addresses of motor-vehicle owners to the highest bidder. A 1967 Valiant owner, Corliss Lamont, sued to prevent the state from selling his name. His suit was dismissed by a U.S. District Judge who stated that the state's revenue-raising technique "may not be the most inspired kind of government function but the information sold is not vital or intimate. It is, moreover, in the category of 'public records,' available to anyone upon demand." The judge claimed that there was no invasion of privacy. "The mailbox, however noxious its advertising contents often seem to judges as well as other people, is hardly the kind of enclave that requires

constitutional defense to protect 'the privacies of life.' The
short though regular journey from mailbox to trash can is an
acceptable burden, at least so far as the Constitution is concerned. And the bells at the door and on the telephone, though
their ring is a more imperious nuisance than the mailman's
tidings," constitute merely "peripheral assaults."[29]

One of the many federal agencies concerned with the inroads of computer technology is the Federal Communications
Commission. On November 10, 1966, they announced prep-
arations for an inquiry dealing with regulatory and policy
problems of computers and communication services. On the
problem of information privacy they stated:

> The modern application of computer technology has
> brought about a trend toward concentrating commercial
> and personal data at computer centers. This concentra-
> tion, resulting in the ready availability in one place of
> detailed personal and business data, raises serious prob-
> lems of how this information can be kept from unauthor-
> ized persons or unauthorized use.
>
> Privacy, particularly in the area of communications, is
> a well established policy and objective of the Communi-
> cations Act. Thus, any threatened or potential invasion
> of privacy is cause for concern by the Commission and
> the industry. In the past, the invasion of information
> privacy was rendered difficult by the scattered and ran-
> dom nature of individual data. Now the fragmentary
> nature of information is becoming a relic of the past. Data
> centers and common memory drums housing competitive
> sales, inventory and credit information and untold amounts
> of personal information, are becoming common. This per-
> sonal and proprietary information must remain free from
> unauthorized invasion or disclosure, whether at the com-
> puter, the terminal station, or the interconnecting com-
> munication link.
>
> Both the developing industry and the Commission must
> be prepared to deal with the problems promptly so that
> they may be resolved in an effective manner before tech-
> nological advances render solution more difficult. The

Commission is interested not only in promoting the development of technology, but it is at the same time concerned that in the process technology does not erode fundamental values.[30]

The centralization of all files into a variety of data banks requires new safeguards because of the increasing ability to tap files and the sensitive nature of data stored in them. Even the Supreme Court has been caught in a two-way struggle. Justice Brennan, in the Lopez case, warned that the court's general decisions on protection of privacy against physical intrusions had "been outflanked by the technological advances of the very recent past," and that unless the courts meet the challenge head on, "we shall be contributing to a climate of official lawlessness and contempt."[31]

The issue has reached worldwide dimensions. Recently seventy-four distinguished American authorities on international law and world politics, members of a private research agency, described in a report the potential threat to individual freedom posed by computers and other electronic devices. This group, the Commission to Study the Organization of Peace, urged that the United Nations "study the implications of scientific and technological developments for human rights and fundamental freedoms and recommend procedures for making the experience of each country available to other countries."[32]

The commission's report said, "There is a cumulative danger involved in the merry march of technology and science without adequate consideration of the social effects of their findings." Noting modern man's growing dependence on computers, the writers declared: "There is a grave danger that actual decisions will be no longer in the hands of the duly elected representatives of the people but instead in the hands of those who feed the data to the computers on which decisions are based and who are the interpreters and implementers of the answers given by the computers."[33]

The study went on to plead that attempts be made to anticipate the sort of dangers to human rights that may emerge and to prepare to meet them. "What is going to happen to human rights in a world which is becoming so complicated that more and more important decisions have to depend on computers and other machines? . . . Many military decisions already depend on answers given by computers, and many experts are working hard on programming computers for work in many crucial areas where decisions might directly impinge on the well-being of vast groups of individuals. Before they go too far, new safeguards need to be developed to protect the rights of individuals and of their elected representatives."[34]

Calling on man to test his ingenuity, the authors said: "New arrangements will have to be devised to control the precious few who know how to run the machines, and on whose wisdom and impartiality the fate of mankind may depend."[35]

The relevancy of the original laws of the land to today's technology has to be re-examined. Certainly we have failed the expectations of the writers of the Constitution by taking too many risks in our reinterpretation of what is meant by privacy and confidence. Robert H. Bahner, Archivist of the United States, said in testimony before the Senate Subcommittee on Administrative Practice and Procedure: "Mr. Chairman, when our Government was in its infancy Thomas Jefferson warned that 'eternal vigilance is the price of liberty.' In our own day, as the Government finds it necessary to accumulate even greater amounts of information about the individual, we believe that Jefferson's admonition has as great a validity as when he made it. One of the earmarks of a free society is the concern of the government for the rights of its citizens, and not the least of these is the right of the individual to expect that during his lifetime information secured in confidence will be kept in confidence."[36]

Some have demanded that work be halted on the creation of a federal data center. Lawrence Speiser, Director of the American Civil Liberties Union office in Washington, D.C., is one. He has said that ". . . the stake here is large; the right of a free people to remain free, unencumbered by the knowledge that for each individual, Big Brother has an electronic file collecting every tidbit of information. There would be no escape. No mistakes would ever be undone. Skeletons in the closets would always be there, only they would be compactly and efficiently transformed into eternal electrical impulses on tape. . . . Efficiency is not the only hallmark of good government. There are other values in a society dedicated to the most comprehensive right of its citizens, 'the right to be let alone.' "[37]

As computer networks and data banks spread throughout the country and world, science and privacy must be able to thrive together. We will be collecting thousands of facts about everyone, depositing these details into the unforgetting computers of the future. As Dr. Westin warns: "Unless the issue of privacy is in the forefront of the planning and administration of future computer systems, the possibilities of data surveillance over the individual in 1984 could be chilling."[38] Unless we are looking for a nation of people who are afraid to speak freely, act in accordance with conscience, and respect the system that they live by, further proof that our Constitution and Bill of Rights still apply is needed. The original Bill of Rights has been expanded by other amendments over the past two hundred years. It could be done again. Supreme Court Justice Douglas in his discussion on liberty stated: "The fences have been broken down. . . . The Bill of Rights—with the judicial gloss it has acquired—plainly is not adequate to protect the individual against the growing bureaucracy."[39]

CHAPTER IX

The Transistorized
Sherlock Holmes

The fear of the impact of technology is sometimes expressed hysterically: "Computers will treat a person like a robot, identify all that there is about him; make him naked and defenseless to the outside world; ultimately determine his job, salary and mate."

A more sophisticated concern is that large-scale, computerized data banks will tend to invade privacy and individuality and accelerate the pressures toward depersonalization and conformity. Error has always demanded forgiveness from the community; until recently limited systems-capability has made it more likely that others would forget and therefore forgive. These factors will be considerably varied by future computerized data systems.

In *The Year 2000*, Kahn and Wiener commented: ". . . computers may also be able to apply a great deal of inferential logic on their own—they may become a sort of transistorized Sherlock Holmes making hypotheses and investigating leads in a more or less autonomous or self-motivated manner, all the while improving their techniques as they accumulate information about patterns of criminal behavior—or any other kind of behavior that authorities decide ought to be observed. New legal doctrines will need to be developed to regulate these new possibilities for 'just looking.' "[1]

There is also concern that even if collections of certain data were sanctioned, the problem of leakage remains. Why aren't appropriate technical protections available today to prevent possible leakage of personal data? Basically, it is a question of economics. Engineering changes to provide necessary insulations would entail a more complex computer system. The chances are that these technical safeguards can be built into the computer, but they will have to be paid for. The increased cost would be passed on to the computer consumer, and in an extremely competitive field, computer manufacturers have been reluctant to take this step.

What happens if these safeguards are not included in the system? Law enforcement agencies have long known that underground organizations sufficiently interested in tapping a file or even a complex system have done so by paying off employees. Organized crime might seek to break into any data system in order to acquire information. Legitimate agencies could also use data from computerized banks—newspapers, private investigators, credit agencies, foreign governments, etc. Vance Packard gives a price list for "confidential" personal data—arrest records at $10, credit reports to non-subscribers at $5 or $10; the going rate for a view of someone else's tax return is at minimum $1,000 since there is danger of legal prosecution.[2]

A frequently heard argument for a national data center quotes the anticipated savings that would result from the sharing of computer installations. Some researchers claim that a centralized data system would assist in projecting the economy and would aid in the design of motivational, sociological and psychological inquiry. As one specialist put it, the government could make available very detailed analyses of consumer purchasing patterns; this would permit more closely controlled production of consumer goods, which would lower prices and lessen business fluctuations.

Experts claim that computers operating within the government would be more objective and efficient than inadequately trained clerks.

On the negative side, Stanley Rothman of TRW Systems Company, a leading technical specialist in the field, points to some fears that may persist about a national data center: "Some government information systems presently depend upon a voluntary supply of information by the populace. Should such a system become really threatening to the populace, these voluntary sources would dry up in some degree." In addition, certain errors are more likely to occur because of an oversimplification of statements in a person's file. A general statement about an individual could easily be interpreted by various employers in a variety of ways. The possibility of error, in fact, increases rather than decreases since so much more collecting is done. Errors could be caused by confusion of a person's identity. "Changes or deletions in the files either intentional or inadvertent would have tremendous consequences. For example, and this is something of an oversimplification, a person could effectively cease to exist because his file was lost. There could be inadvertent libels through procedural mistakes," Rothman points out, and "strictly digital information without signatures or seals is easily copied, counterfeited and transmitted."[3]

The most threatening aspect of government computerized systems is their relation to absolute political power: The government might eventually be able to carry a complete profile on every person in this country. There are penalties for public disclosure. The Civil Rights Act of 1964 prohibits gathering data on race, creed, color and, most recently, sex. In spite of the federal laws restricting distribution of confidential information, there is little that limits the transfer of information *within* the government.

Some structuring as to who should have access to data has already started with the Freedom of Information Law, enacted by Congress in 1966, which established eight categories of "sensitive" government data exempt from disclosure. These are

> . . . defense or foreign-policy secrets authorized to be kept secret by executive order; matters which relate solely

to internal personnel rules and practices of an agency; matters specifically exempted from disclosure by statute; trade secrets and other types of commercial information obtained from the public which are privileged or confidential; inter-agency or intra-agency memoranda or letters dealing solely with matters of law or policy which would not be available by law to a private party in litigation with the agency; personnel and medical and similar matters "the disclosure of which would constitute a clearly unwarranted invasion of personal privacy"; investigatory files compiled for law-enforcement purposes except to the extent available by law to a private party; geological and geophysical data concerning wells; and certain reports prepared for regulating or supervising financial institutions."[4]

An individual who is denied such data can now bring legal action against a government department and the agency must justify its refusal to release data that is not provided for under the act; the agency can be penalized if the act is not complied with. Regarding the public's "right to know," the Senate Judiciary Committee said that the act ". . . enunciates a policy that will involve a balancing of interests between the protection of an individual's private affairs from unnecessary public scrutiny, and the preservation of the public's right to governmental information. The application of this policy should lend itself particularly to those government agencies where persons are forced to submit vast accounts of personal data usually for limited purpose such as health, welfare, and selective service records."[5]

Although the act provides considerable protection, there is no provision for challenging the release by a department, to the public or to any other department, of information that the citizen himself judges to be private.

In addition, the American public is faced with bureaucratic intrusion. According to former Senator Edward Long ". . . there are more than 30,000 federal investigators, most of them dedicated men whose records are exemplary," but, ". . . some of these men, unaware that they are servants of the people, have intimidated, threatened and harassed individuals and groups. . . . Some have used police state techniques. Bureaucracy is inherent in big government, and such trespasses are not easy to correct. In the quagmire of red tape and official procedures, the significance of the individual's rights tends to sink, often without a trace."[6]

The policy of the different states varies considerably. Nineteen states provide privacy rights by law, but some do not. Some states prohibit the unauthorized use of the name, portrait or picture of a living person in advertising or trade. Georgia, perhaps, has the broadest statement of this principle in law: "Privacy is derived from natural law and is an inalienable right."[7]

There are complicated legal questions relating to data collection. What is the authority over federal-state-city exchange of personal data? At what point does national security take precedence over confidentiality? Does voluntary commitment by a sex deviate, narcotic addict, institutionalized incompetent person, etc., waive the right to privacy? What rights exist for juveniles, ex-convicts, seniles, welfare dependents, wards of the state? Can the information collected by computers be used as court evidence? When is a file so thorough that it reads just like a personal diary? The fourth amendment in the Bill of Rights, "The right of the people to be secure in their . . . papers . . . against unreasonable searches and seizures . . ." may suggest the need to have a search warrant to look at a person's file. Assuming that such a dossier is used in court proceedings, in what situations can it be altered, and what forms of legal ruling would be required to change or even withdraw certain information from an individual's file?

The Lockheed Missiles and Space Company, under contract to the State of California, studied the legal problems involved in designing a state-wide data system. They identified the following legal areas that demand further research:

(1) Exchanges of information that are prohibited by statute, such as the disclosure of adoption proceedings; (2) Exchanges that are at an administrator's discretion, such as public health transmission of venereal disease cases to the police department; (3) The class of privileged

communications, such as those between doctor and patient, that a state collects through its hospital systems; (4) The immunity and liability laws relating to individual government employees and government itself.[8]

To date there are no adequate legal protections to safeguard the individual against computer leakage. Furthermore, laws alone will not offer satisfactory protection in the face of widespread use of these systems. Although laws can impose penalties for violation and can set the limits of proper safeguards, legislative actions have not always been effective in the control of surveillance activities like wiretapping and eavesdropping.

There is reason to hesitate before passing new legislation that might in fact backfire. Laws that give special agencies or departments the responsibility of investigating those who break the law would be introducing yet other bodies that decide who can know what, thus putting a new decision-power in the hands of a few.

One of the foremost spokesmen on the issue of privacy, Alan Westin of Columbia University, believes that legislative bodies should ". . . adopt as their guiding principle, the concept that an individual's right to limit the circulation of personal information about himself is a vital ingredient of his right to privacy and this should not be infringed without showing of strong social need and the satisfaction of requirements for protective safeguards."

We have to make sure that information given to a specific agency will not be shared in such a way that the person's identity will be discovered. It is necessary to specify those who may use certain technological devices. Neither the principal of a school nor a personnel director should be allowed to enter at will the dossier on a potential or present student or employee. The question of duration of surveillance is most important. In addition, we need to determine what kinds of electronic devices are appropriate and permissible.

We must define the penalties that would be imposed on those who disclose information improperly or without authorization, and we must regulate the use of information for purposes other than that for which it was originally obtained. Westin suggests:

> The effective use of computers calls for a rational analysis and painstaking planning; the growth in personal-data processing will necessitate the same high levels of analysis and planning by federal and state legislatures if privacy is to survive. This means that fresh studies ought to be made of existing confidentiality and nondisclosure requirements for information acquired by government agencies in their regulatory and data collecting roles. Provisions for confidentiality of information, restrictions on improper circulation, and sanctions against unauthorized use should be written into the basic legislation and administrative rules governing the new law enforcement computer systems. Similar legislative action is desirable for the government data centers that are rapidly coming into operation at both state and federal levels.
>
> As the computerization process expands, legislatures might consider the wisdom of a statute applying the same "common law" approach in this area as in the psychological and physical surveillance fields. Such a statute might contain a broad classification that information given to the government for a specific purpose may not be used for any other purpose or given further circulation unless the identity of individual or group supplying the information is completely removed from the data, or the supplying source freely consents to the additional circulation. Further exception might be made for a small class of situations requiring either limited or general circulation in the government's discretion. The independent agency previously described might also be assigned responsibility for adjudicating complaints from citizens or government employees about misuse of personal and confidential information.[9]

Two additional laws might be useful at this point. One would prohibit some federal departments from asking certain kinds of questions. This would fall into the realm of questions related to religion, free speech, or personal matters. Another would allow persons to know who said what about them in order to question or rebut. Protections must be established within the framework of the public consensus. Unfortunately people will sometimes find justification for acts of invasion of privacy.

We must also bear in mind that we are dealing with a super-technology that will become increasingly complex and difficult to evaluate. It is safe to assume that probably the only persons who will understand the complexities and operations of these systems will be the computer designers and systems engineers who are directly responsible for the evolution of the industry.

Safeguards can be inserted into a system already in use, but it would be more efficient and less costly to build them in at the time the computer is designed. The burden of a great deal of the responsibility must lie with the computer manufacturers. If they want to avoid external regulation, they will have to start thinking about how to design systems with built-in safeguards.

Computer manufacturers should provide minimal cryptographic protections to modify the signals so that they may not easily be deciphered by a wiretapper. These protections would be connected to all communications wires that carry information from data banks. This does not imply the need for an overly complex design, but rather a basic operation upon the stream of information to make the job of invasion more difficult than it is worth. Although a cryptographic code is not a hundred per cent foolproof, it does act as a delaying tactic that may make the data less useful to the invader. Data could be modified so that even if an unauthorized person read out the contents of the computer, he would not automatically have access to confidential matter.

Another shield could be a "passkey" device which accepts only properly authorized users. There might be a card with coded punch holes indicating both the kind and amount of information to which the person holding the card should have access. (There is of course the possibility of loss or theft of such a passkey.)

In sections of the government defense system, clearance is given only when two authorized requests are made by different people.

There has been talk of developing proper protections in larger installations by a "criss-cross" system, which would have several memory units, each containing data which would have to be pieced together before access could be achieved. It would be more difficult to tap the entire system without proper authorization.

Speech recognition can also be employed to protect confidential data. Research has shown that distinctive acoustical patterns of different voices can be used as a safeguard. Built into a computer, a voice-recognition unit could challenge any unauthorized voice.

A random review of banks should be standard practice in order to insure that no individual machine operator or programmer can use an acceptable password. A secret trap door would guard against a clever programmer who might slip a couple of complex instructions into the computer to signal it to give him the password.

Paul Baran of the RAND Corporation suggests that mechanisms are needed to pinpoint unusual data requests. Thus if an individual or group requested a certain specific type of data too often, the computer would become "suspicious" and make a notation asking for human investigation of the situation.[10]

Probably the best example of how protection measures could be incorporated into a vast communication network is the telephone system.

Known only too well to many of us, our home telephones are constantly deluged with crank calls, unsolicited advertising, threats of one kind or another, false alarms and obscene messages. For many, an immediate response has been a withdrawal from the public by unlisted numbers or merely initials to avoid sexual identity. In our Federal capital, these calls became so out of hand that Congress raised the penalty for making obscene calls from $10 to $500. To be sure rarely is a person making an obscene telephone call ever found, which points up the limits of legal action. In all probability, it should be the responsibility of the telephone systems across the nation to technologically provide more safeguards. For example, should you receive such a call, you should be able to merely press a button attached to your unit thereby creating a bridge to a bank of records at a neighborhood police station. Once a teletypewriter identifies the name, address and telephone number of the calling party, a quick call to a stand-by car would get many of these callers arrested. Although it would be more expensive to design, install and make operational such a system, the end result would be telephone safeguards that would form added protection to prevent it from being socially misused.[11]

At M.I.T., in addition to requiring the computer user to carry identification, there are hardware locks that prevent execution, reading, or modification of information.

Bernard Peters, of the National Security Agency in Fort Meade, Maryland, has suggested ways of limiting the possibility of leakage. Computerized data banks could be monitored by an appropriate authority: "The monitor is the key defense, the key security element in the system. . . . Monitors for multiprogramming need a high degree of program and file integrity to be effective." Peters goes on to say:

> The monitor must manage the system clocks and the main console. If the maintenance panel is beyond management by the monitor, it must be secured . . . the monitor must be carefully designed to limit the amount of critical coding. When an interrupt occurs, control is transferred to the monitor and the core is unprotected. The monitor, must, as soon as reasonable, adjust the memory bounds to provide limits on even the monitor's own coding.
>
> The monitor must be adequately tested. It is certainly necessary to adequately demonstrate the security capability to the governing authority. In addition to passing its initial acceptance the monitor must also test itself

continuously. For instance, the memory bounds protection can be expected to fail with some probability.

What is the monitor to do if there is a violation? If there is a violation of the memory bounds or the use of a privileged instruction by a user program, the monitor must immediately suspend the offending program and must make log entries. It must also prohibit the further use of the offending program by the user submitting the violating program until specifically authorized by a supervisor. The suspension of violating program requests must be thorough and complete. If the task has been divided into multiple concurrent operating activities, all such activities must be terminated. If the task has resulted in a chain of requests, all such requests must be removed from the queue. Violation of security rules by any activity must result in a complete abort of all parts of that request. This is necessary to prevent a user program from making multiple tries against the security system.

Security rules cannot be suspended for debugging or program testing. It is clear that security rules cannot be suspended for debugging programs because the new program is the one most likely to violate security. The debugging system must live with the security restrictions although some concessions can be made for debugging. For example, one can flag a program that is in a debugging state. Then if a bounds violation occurs, the system could merely log it and send a dump of the program to the user rather than sounding a major alarm.[12]

It should be remembered that Peters is addressing himself mainly to security problems, which are not necessarily parallel to issues of invasion of privacy. Security data are protected against leakage by the federal government. As Willis Ware of the RAND Corporation said: "Legal foundations for protecting classified information are well established, whereas in the privacy situation a uniform authority over users and a penalty structure for infractions are lacking."[13]

To date, the best attempt to identify the relationships between computer surveillance and invasion of privacy has been outlined by Petersen and Turn of the RAND Corporation.[14] They visualize two types of disclosures of information—accidental disclosures resulting from failure within the computer, and deliberate disclosures from infiltration of the system. Deliberate invasion can be either passive or active. The former is accomplished by wiretapping or some other electronic pickup system. The latter is accomplished by direct access procedures—browsing around the files, pretending to be an authorized seeker of data, using the computer as an authorized staff member, e.g., programmer, operator, manager, maintenance man. The following table summarizes these measures:

Nature of Infiltration	Means	Effects
Accidental	Computer malfunctioning; user errors, undebugged programs	Privileged information dumped at wrong terminals, print-outs, etc.
Deliberate passive	Wiretapping, electromagnetic pickup, examining carbon paper	User's interest in information revealed; content of communications revealed
Deliberate active	Entering files by: "browsing," "masquerading," "between-lines"	Specific information revealed or modified as a result of infiltrator's actions

Petersen and Turn suggest countermeasures to prevent surveillance of data within a computerized system or computerized data bank. The chart on pages 174–176 summarizes their approach. It is a table that should command considerable attention from the computer manufacturers while the government is still willing to allow the business community the time and leadership to rectify some shortcomings.

Unfortunately, essential safeguards are not as easily attained as is suggested by some of these outspoken specialists. It is one thing to design countermeasures as they apply to the "general" concept of computer leakage; it is quite another matter to build in protections for a specific computerized system.

SUMMARY OF COUNTERMEASURES TO THREAT TO INFORMATION PRIVACY

COUNTERMEASURE / THREAT	Access Control (passwords, authentication, authorization)	Processing Restrictions (storage, protect, privileged operations)	Privacy Transformations	Threat Monitoring (audits, logs)	Integrity Management (hardware, software, personnel)
Accidental:					
User error	Good protection, unless the error produces correct password	Reduce susceptibility	No protection if depend on password; otherwise, good protection	Identifies the "accident prone"; provides *post facto* knowledge of possible loss	Not applicable
System error	Good protection, unless bypassed due to error	Reduce susceptibility	Good protection in case of communication system switching errors	May help in diagnosis or provide *post facto* knowledge	Minimizes possibilities for accidents
Deliberate, passive:					
Electromagnetic pick-up	No protection	No protection	Reduces susceptibility; work factor determines the amount of protection	No protection	Reduces susceptibility
Wiretapping	No protection	No protection	Reduces susceptibility; work factor	No protection	If applied to communication circuits may reduce

			determines the amount of protection		susceptibility
Waste Basket	Not applicable	Not applicable	Not applicable	Not applicable	Proper disposal procedures
Deliberate, active: "Browsing"	Good protection (may make masquerading necessary)	Reduces ease to obtain desired information	Good protection	Identifies unsuccessful attempts; may provide *post facto* knowledge or operate real-time alarms	Aides other counter-measures
"Masquerading"	Must know authenticating passwords (work factor to obtain these)	Reduces ease to obtain desired information	No protection if depends on password; otherwise, sufficient	Identifies unsuccessful attempts; may provide *post facto* knowledge or operate real-time alarms	Makes harder to obtain information for masquerading; since masquerading is deception, may inhibit browsers
"Between lines" entry	No protection unless used for every message	Limits the infiltrator to the same potential as the user whose line he shares	Good protection if privacy transformation changed in less time than required by work factor	*Post facto* analysis of activity may provide knowledge of possible loss	Communication network integrity helps
"Piggy-back" entry	No protection but reverse (processor-to-user) authentication may help	Limits the infiltrator to the same potential as the user whose line he shares	Good protection if privacy transformation changed in less time than required by work factor	*Post facto* analysis of activity may provide knowledge of possible loss	Communication network integrity helps

SUMMARY OF COUNTERMEASURES TO THREAT TO INFORMATION PRIVACY—Continued

COUNTERMEASURE / THREAT	Access Control (passwords, authentication, authorization)	Processing Restrictions (storage, protect, privileged operations)	Privacy Transformations	Threat Monitoring (audits, logs)	Integrity Management (hardware, software, personnel)
Entry by system personnel	May have to masquerade	Reduces ease of obtaining desired information	Work factor, unless depend on password and masquerading is successful	Post facto analysis of activity may provide knowledge of possible loss	Key to the entire privacy protection system
Entry via "trap doors"	No protection	Probably no protection	Work factor, unless access to keys obtained	Possible alarms, post facto analysis	Protection through initial verification and subsequent maintenance of hardware and software integrity
Core dumping to get residual information	No protection	Erase private core areas at swapping time	No protection unless encoded processing feasible	Possible alarms, post facto analysis	Not applicable
Physical acquisition of removable files	Not applicable	Not applicable	Work factor, unless access to keys obtained	Post facto knowledge form audits of personnel movements	Physical preventive measures and devices

For example, few can find fault with Petersen and Turn's countermeasures but they are merely a theoretical framework for the complex changes that are needed. These counter-measures offer little assistance to those attempting to design a surveillance-proof computerized data-bank in the medical field, in an educational community, for a corporation or for a federal repository.

Examples of a specific computer utilization within a defined framework are necessary. The rules that apply for one data bank might be inadequate for another or might fail to respond to the more crucial or pressing needs.

Before adequate safeguards can be developed, a decision must be made about what sort of disclosure is appropriate. Under what conditions should a child's IQ or personality scores be released to a teacher, school administrator, parent or, for that matter, to the student himself? Under what conditions should a medical record be made available to a patient's family, doctor, employer, clergyman or even the patient? Under what conditions should a citizen's income tax earnings over the past five years be released to another federal agency, the state or city government, a member of the FBI, a credit bank or the university scholarship committee reviewing his son's request for financial aid?

No two data banks will be identical. Each in its own way will require a detailed systems analysis. No "off the shelf" safeguards will satisfy the earnest engineers, lawyers and citizens determined to come up with the best protections that money, good reasoning and a liberal philosophy can buy.

Some of the best thinking on protection of confidentiality and safeguards against computer leakage has been presented by Arthur Miller:

> To ensure freedom from governmental intrusion, Congress must legislate reasonably precise standards regarding the information that can be recorded in the National Data Center. Certain types of information should not be recorded even if it is technically feasible to do so and a legitimate administrative objective exists. For example, it has long been "feasible," and from some vantage points "desirable," to require citizens to carry and display pass-

ports when traveling in this country, or to require universal fingerprinting. But we have not done so because these encroachments on our liberties are deemed inconsistent with the philosophical fiber of our society. Likewise, highly personal information, especially medical and psychiatric information, should not be permitted in the center unless human life depends upon recording it.

Legislation sharply limiting the information which federal agencies and officials can extract from private citizens is absolutely essential. To reinforce these limitations, the statute creating the Data Center should prohibit recording any information collected without specific congressional authorization. Until the quality of the center's operations and the nature of its impact on individual privacy can be better perceived, the center's activities should be restricted to the preservation of factual data.

Miller clearly identified the two principal types of needed safeguards: those for upholding the validity of the stored data, and those for controlling the distribution of information within the system.

To ensure the accuracy of the center's files, an individual should have an opportunity to correct errors in information concerning him. Perhaps a print-out of his computer file should be sent to him once a year. Admittedly, this process would be expensive; some agencies will argue that the value of certain information will be lost if it is known that the government has it; and there might be squabbles between citizens and the Data Center concerning the accuracy of the file that would entail costly administrative proceedings. Nonetheless, the right of a citizen to be protected against governmental dissemination of misinformation is so important that we must be willing to pay some price to preserve it. Instead of an annual mailing, citizens could be given access to their files on request, perhaps through a network of remote computer terminals situated in government buildings throughout the country. What is necessary is a procedure for periodically determining when data are outmoded or should be removed from the file.

The expense could be reduced if a print-out of collated data was sent out with each income-tax form at the beginning of the year. This would prove to be not only a relatively inexpensive way of disseminating the data, but a technically feasible operation as well, since address labels for the tax books are prepared by computers.

Turning to the question of access, the center's computer hardware and software must be designed to limit access to the information. A medical history given to a government doctor in connection with an application for veteran's benefits should not be available to federal employees not legitimately involved in processing the application. One solution may be to store information according to its sensitivity or its accessibility, or both. Then, governmental officials can be assigned access keys that will let them reach only those portions of the center's files that are relevant to their particular governmental function.

Everyone directing an inquiry to the center or seeking to deposit information in it should be required to identify himself. Finger-or-voice-prints ultimately may be the best form of identification. As snooping techniques become more sophisticated, systems may even be needed to counter the possibility of forgery or duplication; perhaps an answer-back system or a combination of finger-and-voice prints will be necessary. In addition, the center should be equipped with protector files to record the identity of inquirers, and these files should be audited to unearth misuse of the system. It probably will also be necessary to audit the programs controlling the manipulation of the files and access to the system to make sure that no one has inserted a secret "door" or a password permitting entry to the data by unauthorized personnel. It is frightening to realize that at present there apparently is no foolproof way to prevent occasional "monitor intrusion" in large data-processing systems. Additional protection against these risks can be achieved by exercising great care in selecting programming personnel.

In the future, sophisticated connections between the center and federal offices throughout the country and between the federal center and numerous state, local and private centers probably will exist. As a result, information will move into and out of the center over substantial distances by telephone lines or microwave relays. The center's "network" character will require information to be protected against wiretapping and other forms of electronic eavesdropping. Transmission in the clear undoubtedly will have to be proscribed, and data in machine-readable form will have to be scrambled or further encoded so that they can be rendered intelligible only by a decoding process built into the system's authorized terminals. Although it may not be worth the effort or expense to develop completely breakproof codes, sufficient scrambling or coding to make it expensive for an eavesdropper to intercept the center's transmission will be necessary. If information in the center is arranged according to sensitivity or accessibility, the most efficient procedure may be to use codes of different degrees of complexity.

At a minimum, congressional action is necessary to establish the appropriate balance between the needs of the national government in accumulating, processing, and disseminating information and the right of individual privacy. This legislation must be reinforced by statutory civil remedies and penal sanctions.

The question of who should have control of a data center in the national government is still to be debated. Should an existing agency be empowered with this new administrative responsibility, or should a new department be specifically established, perhaps reporting directly to the appropriate cabinet secretary?

. . . it would be folly to leave the center in the hands of any agency whose employees are known to engage in antiprivacy activities. Similarly, the center must be kept away from government officials who are likely to become so entranced with operating sophisticated machinery and manipulating large masses of data that they will not respect an individual's right to privacy.

The conclusion seems inescapable: control over the center must be lodged outside existing channels. A new, completely independent agency, bureau, or office should be established—perhaps as an adjunct to the Census Bureau or the National Archives—to formulate policy under whatever legislative guidelines are enacted to ensure the privacy of all citizens. The organization would operate the center, regulate the nature of the information that can be recorded and stored, ensure its accuracy, and protect the center against breaches of security.

The new agency's ability to avoid becoming a captive of the governmental units using the center would be crucial. Perhaps with proper staffing and well-delineated lines of authority to Congress or the President, the center could achieve the degree of independence needed to protect individuals against governmental or private misuse of information in the center. At the other end of the spectrum, the center cannot become an island unto itself, populated by technocrats whose conduct is shielded by the alleged omniscience of the machines they manage and who are neither responsive nor responsible to anyone.[15]

Prior to the formal establishment of a federal data bank, an appropriate structure should be developed in the form of a superagency composed of representatives from government, law, the social sciences, public interest, computer sciences, corporations and the bank's users. At the outset, they should review any of the proposed data-bank legislation and, after considerable study and approval, submit their recommendations to Congress. Before they approve the bank, they must be satisfied that only summary tabulations of data will be included, in which individuals' names are protected against leakage, and that appropriate safeguards exist. Should a data repository be established, this group would remain responsible for the physical operation of the bank; the procedures for selecting those who will survey the computers; the decision on what data can be stored and retrieved; the control of validity; and the perennial watch for data leakage.

The senior staff of this new agency should be selected by the President or a delegated member of his Cabinet, to whom the chairman of the agency would then report directly. The salaried members of this staff should be given the authority to stop any person and challenge his right to retrieve data, and should be empowered to take legal action when a violation occurs.

A standing Congressional subcommittee would at all times have the option to review procedures and consider those complaints from the public that were not satisfactorily resolved by the agency itself.

Membership in the agency's top leadership should be limited —perhaps to five years—to prevent complacency or relaxation. Replacements, for the same reason, should be made from outside the agency. To ensure competence and continuity, changes should be made on a rotated period of service, i.e., a term of two years, a term of three years. Finally, support staff should receive security clearance before appointment to the agency.

Various safeguards should also be considered for the computerized data systems of nongovernmental organizations. Inevitably, as more and more industries computerize and employ time-sharing devices, their files will become vulnerable to leakage, either by accident or on purpose. With sophisticated advances in technology, one corporation may find that its secrets have become known to a competing industry. If not brought within the domain of legal protections, data stored by credit bureaus, insurance companies, educational institutions, hospitals and agencies of local and state governments will invite attempts at surveillance and intrusion. Miller continues:

> Congress should consider the need for legislation setting standards to be met by nonfederal computer organizations in providing information about private persons and restraining federal officers from access to certain types of information from nonfederal data centers. Nonfederal systems should be required to install some protective devices and procedures. This is not to suggest that Congress

should necessarily impose the same controls on nonfederal systems that it may choose to impose on the federal center. But a protector file to record the source of inquiries and modest encoding would probably prevent wide-scale abuse, although security needs vary from system to system. Since security may be facilitated by installing protective devices in the computer hardware itself, the possible need for regulation of certain aspects of computer manufacturing also should be taken into account.[16]

Even if these anticipated safeguards are incorporated as a permanent control, we should not become complacent. Although these protections may be adequate today, with greater power of computers and technological innovation over the next decades it can be expected that new ways will be found to penetrate the present system. At all times, we must be prepared to improve our protections.

:

There are certain general rules of conduct—pertaining to *all* computerized data banks—that should be followed in order to increase confidentiality and reduce information leakage:

1. Let people know what their records contain, how they are used and protected, and who has access to them.
2. Employ a verification process to insure accuracy of data; in addition, permit the individual to review the data for accuracy, completeness, current application, and freedom from bias.
3. Categorize all stored information as intimate, private and therefore non-circulating (such as physical, psychiatric or credit information); pertinent, but confidential and having limited distribution; or public, and therefore freely distributed.
4. Regard personal data as personal property, requiring permission for its use, and punishing its improper use.
5. Appointing an ombudsman agency—or a committee that represents all levels of the organization—to take major responsibility for hearing and responding to

complaints, and to determine appropriate measures to minimize leakage.
6. Record each request for access that is made, along with the authorization.
7. Make security checks on computer personnel.
8. Assess, from time to time, people's attitudes toward and anxieties about the issue of invasion of privacy. Such studies could be used as a basis for determining what form of records would be most acceptable.
9. Periodically review and update the adequacy of the physical safeguards. Employ capable outside consultants to attest to the safety of the systems used, and to assist in the development of appropriate technical devices (such as scrambled data and code names).
10. Exempt the files from a court's subpoena.
11. Allow psychological seclusion and withdrawal from accountability to remain as a permanent stronghold of our value system. The individual must freely choose whether or not he wishes to become submissive to the power of the system.

A creative response by the computer industry to its technology will probably serve, and satisfy, the public better than rewriting our laws. In fact, one can doubt that legal measures —although necessary—will be as effective as technological adjustments in the protection of the public's privacy.

In terms of priorities, it appears that before Congress proceeds to restructure existing laws or write new ones, it should allow a period of time to pass in order to allow the computer experts to "clean up their own house." This approach is in keeping with our national tradition of not permitting the government to interfere with the control of an operation without first allowing those involved to present recommendations and make amends as they see fit. Once the computer manufacturers have fulfilled their obligation, then the burden of responsibility is transferred to the organizations utilizing the systems to guarantee the fullest security and safeguards against data leakage.

What is needed before the establishment of a *federal* data

bank is a rigorous research effort to answer the following
unresolved questions:

1. What are the purposes of a computerized central facility? What kinds of information are strictly relevant to
   these purposes?
2. How much information about an individual is required to guarantee that such services are useful to
   the person, community and nation? How accurate,
   objective and challengeable is the information?
3. What are the procedures for interagency cooperation
   in the data bank?
4. How will individuals be protected from the creation
   and distribution of derogatory data caused by clerical
   mistakes or computer malfunction?
5. Will procedures be developed to permit individuals to
   see their files?
6. Will the cost of such a facility be justified in terms of
   future savings?
7. Will there be adequate safeguards to prevent penetration from the outside?
8. In whose backyard should this data bank be physically established?
9. Will a bank officially created as a statistical center
   eventually become a storehouse of personal information?
10. Does the concept of this federal data center suggest
    a changing value system and further government in-
    tervention in the lives of Americans?

   The burden of proof of the security of the data facility
should lie primarily with those who propose it. They must
demonstrate that they can create a virtually unpenetrable and
incorruptible system and justify its greater economy and expanding services.
   Perhaps the best way to begin would be to examine closely
the present "privacy abuses" in governmental data systems.
According to Stanley Rothman, it would be worthwhile to find
out how the following problems are handled at present in the

government computerized world: establishment and maintenance of identity, erroneous data, procedural mistakes, inadvertent disclosure, counterfeit input and output, libelous disclosures, and maintenance of name files.[17]

What is called for is the identification of all the engineering safeguards that might be used. These should be designed and presented on paper in blueprint form. An independent committee should then examine these protections and conduct a "vulnerability study" to determine the possibilities of penetration, and thus provide a judgmental assessment as to the safety aspects that would ultimately be installed.

:

The dialogue has just begun. The right to preserve privacy is a right worth fighting for. A federal data bank and other computerized systems offer great potential for increased efficiency; yet they also present the gravest threat of invasion of our innermost thoughts and actions. As we charge, or are billed for, more and more of the services and goods we buy, all these transactions of our personal movement and financial status will glut the records of our lives and offer a very up-to-date picture of how we conduct ourselves in private. Some see this trend as leading to an Orwellian nightmare with Big Brother watching over us and reporting to the central record-control authorities any behavior adjudged out-of-line with stated policy.

There will undoubtedly someday be a federal data center, to be followed by other massive computerized banks, and computers may prove themselves the worthy servant of man. But the servant must yield to his master, and the necessary thought must be given to developing essential safeguards. The computer manufacturers have thus far shirked their responsibility, but they cannot long remain bystanders if they wish to continue to make their own decisions. Both the manufacturer and then the consumer must seek ways to control the all-documenting, all-remembering computer systems and demonstrate that machine technology need not necessarily bear the stamp of increased surveillance. The editorial in the *New York Times* of August 9, 1966, which dealt with the federal data bank, concluded: "Perhaps in the long run the fight to preserve

privacy is a vain one. But like the struggle to preserve
must be continued while any shred of privacy remains.'

We owe not only to ourselves, but to future generation
protection against disregard for privacy. The ultimate sub
sion must be of the machine to man. If we fail to act immediately to preserve our claims to anonymity, psychological
independence and seclusion, our children and children's children may have cause to condemn us for their very altered way
of life.

APPENDIX

A List of Pertinent Glossary Terms

access time: the period between the request for information from storage and the moment when it is delivered.

ADP: stands for automatic data processing. A system of electronic calculating machines connected in such a way as to reduce the need for manpower and provide the rapid handling of data.

ALGOL: stands for algorithmic oriented language, an international procedure language.

alpha-numeric: a term referring to numbers, digits, letters of the alphabet and other special characters. It describes a capacity of many modern-day computers that were originally limited to the handling of digits.

analog computer: as contrasted with a digital computer, it primarily handles data based on a specific measured input. The data is usually of a continuous nature, like the gradual change in temperature. An analog computer measures continuously, unlike a digital computer, which measures discretely.

Analytical Engine: Charles Babbage's 1833 general purpose computer.

artificial memory: opposite of human memory; any means of storing information that in some way parallels man's effort.

automation: the technology of working, in which the handling methods, processes, and design of the processed material and data are integrated to utilize, as economically as possible, the mechanization of thought and effort, in order to achieve an automatic and, in some cases, self-regulating chain of processes.

auxiliary hardware: equipment or machines not directly tied in with the central processing unit of the computer.

batch processing: the batch is composed of records or files put together as a total unit.

binary: a numbering system based on 2's, using the digits 0 and 1. Differs from the digital system, which is based on 10's.

bionics: a marriage between biology and electronics, whereby what is known about the living system is used to develop appropriate equipment for an electronic system.

bit: the abbreviation for binary digit; a single character in a binary number.

Boolian algebra: devised by the mathematician George Boole, it is like basic algebra but is of particular value in computers employing a binary system.

calculator: a simplified computer that performs arithmetic operations, usually on a manual basis.

central processor: the equipment within a total computer system that possesses the network to control and carry out the input and instructions.

COBOL: stands for common business oriented language. A coding approach in which procedures are outlined in a standard form.

common language: a coding technique that is useful to two or more computers allowing them to directly communicate with each other.

computer: a highly sophisticated calculator that applies a series of processes to data, resulting in an output.

computer-assisted instruction (CAI): a method whereby educational materials are fed into computers, which then "teach" in classroom situations.

console: the part of the computer system that contains the control keys, i.e., start button, stop button, power switch.

converter: a piece of equipment that alters information from one form to another so it can become acceptable to another machine.

cryogenics: an approach to increase computer speed by utilizing changes in materials at temperatures approaching zero.

cybernation: the societal consequences of cybernetics, relating control systems to communications; a term first used by Donald Michael.

cybernetics: a concept introduced by Norbert Wiener; it compares the communication control aspects of machines to capabilities of man's nervous system.

data bank: a file system that holds massive amounts of information, either statistical or informational in nature; may be referred to as data center.

debugging: a way of adjusting or correcting errors or machine malfunctions of programs or computer equipment.

Difference Engine: the predecessor of Charles Babbage's analytical engine; it computes all arithmetic calculations.

digital computer: as contrasted with an analog computer, it performs a series of logical and arithmetic operations, utilizing numbers to express variables of a situation.

disk: a magnetized piece of metal that appears like a phonograph record; it contains information on both sides and can be read by numerous "needle heads." Usually a set of disks are placed in one file.

drum: a cylinder containing a magnetized surface in which data can be placed and stored.

electronic data processing: a process for analyzing data, usually performed by electronic equipment, i.e., computers.

feedback: the returning of a part of a machine's output for ultimate use as a new input.

first-generation computer: introduced in 1950, these were inefficient, massive systems that were powered by vacuum tubes and contained limited memory capacity.

flow chart: a system for graphically illustrating a computer operation or system.

FORTRAN: stands for formula translator, a language described in algebraic format.

general purpose computer: a computer system that can be used to answer a wide range of questions.

GIGO: a slang phrase describing useless, meaningless data— garbage in, garbage out.

hardware: just about any piece of computer equipment, all components of the computer.

heuristic method: simulation of human learning processes by a computer.

hybrid computers: a recent innovation combining analog and digital computers, designed to result in a more efficient, useful system.

information data center: a bank that generates "intelligence" data, information about people; also referred to as an intelligence data center.

input: data taken from a source outside of the computer and subsequently fed into the system.

instruction: a coded rule that instructs the computer to perform one of its functions.

key punch: a piece of equipment used to imprint data on cards or tapes by punching holes representing letters, numbers and special characters.

language: a set of characters that form symbols and instructions for meaningful communication, e.g., COBOL, FORTRAN.

laser: a powerful concentrated beam of light that has numerous applications, one of which will be with computers.

leasing company: an organization that purchases computers from a manufacturer and then proceeds to rent out the equipment, usually on a monthly basis.

magnetic core: a magnetized high-speed storage unit.

magnetic drum: a rotating cylinder with a magnetic surface used to store information.

magnetic tape: a reel of magnetic or plastic tape on which data are recorded for storage. It plays like the tape on high-fidelity equipment.

memory: a synonym in computer language for "storage"; any

piece of equipment in which information is held to be readily available for recall at some future time.

MICR: stands for magnetic ink character recognition. The recognition of data printed with magnetized ink.

microsecond: a millionth of a second.

monitor: a program designed to supervise the operation of routines within a computer.

nanosecond: a billionth of a second.

noise: extraneous or useless information that should be removed from data when the data are ready to be used.

OCR: stands for optical character recognition; enables printed characters to be identified.

optical scanner: a device used to recognize different symbols and characters which are then placed into a control unit for conversion into a language meaningful to the computer.

output: any form of computer results.

patch: means of correcting a mistake, possibly by placing a section of coding into the path to alter a routine.

peripheral equipment: equipment used in cooperation with the computer, but not part of the computer itself, i.e., typewriters, key punches.

photochromism: the ability of certain materials to alter their color under different kinds of light; it has potential to increase storage capacities.

picosecond: a trillionth of a second; a thousandth of a nanosecond.

print-out: a documenting of what is available in a memory unit.

privacy: the right to determine how, when, and to what extent, data about oneself are released to another person.

program: a scheme for an automatic solution to a question or problem; it includes the strategy for obtaining, coding and feeding data into the system.

punch card: a piece of heavy card of predetermined size that is meaningfully punched so as to be readable by equipment within the system.

random-access: the gathering of data in computer memory in which one location of information selected is not related to the location of previously pulled information.

real-time: this is the actual time that a process takes. Usually the time is so short that a person cannot tell the difference between the request for information and the answer.

retrieval: the recall of stored data.

satellite processor: usually a small unit used for conversions from punch card to tape and printing of tape contents.

second generation computer: introduced in 1960, these were transistorized systems that maintained larger storage and employed magnetic tapes.

service bureau: a computer center to which a person can bring raw data to receive appropriate service and analysis.

software: as opposed to hardware, software is the internal program, i.e., languages, assemblers, generators.

solid state: electronic components that carry the electronic flow by means of materials such as crystal diodes, ferrite cores, transistors.

statistical data center: a bank that provides statistical information which cannot be related directly to any one person, group or organization.

storage: any device which retains information; synonymous with "memory."

surveillance: the watching over or supervision of an individual.

system: a collection of interrelated computer components.

tape: used for storing data as input or output for a computer; there are two types—magnetic or paper tape.

teletypewriter: an AT & T trade name referring to telegraph-terminal devices.

terminal: a point where data enters or leaves a computer system.

third-generation computer: introduced in 1964, these transistor-ized systems of micro-electronic circuits have great speeds and increased capacity and flexibility.

time-sharing: use of one device, usually a computer, for two or more purposes at the same time.

total information system: also referred to as integrated in-formation system; a highly sophisticated system permitting maximum control over opera-tions and data, and approaches for better planning.

verify: to compare one file of data with another to minimize error.

Questionnaire on a Federal Data Bank

I. Today, all information that the Government has about people and organizations is on file in numerous departments scattered through-out the country. These files contain records such as income tax, school, social security, employment, criminal and other information about yourself.

While these operations have proven satisfactory in the past, with a growing population and increased Federal activity, the computer now makes it possible to have a more efficient and centralized Gov-ernment. Therefore, a proposal has been made to develop one centralized computer system (a Federal Data Bank) which will be able to collect, store and use information from the major depart-ments of the Government. Ultimately, data on every person and organization will be available at the push of a button.

II. A. What negative or bad effects do you see resulting from a collec-tion of information in a centralized Federal Data Bank?

_____

_____

_____

B. What positive or good effects do you see resulting from a collection of information in a centralized Federal Data Bank?

_____

_____

_____

III. Please react to the following statements by placing a check in the appropriate box, using the scale at the right:

	Agree Strongly	*Agree*	*Neutral*	*Disagree*	*Disagree Strongly*
A. The Government should have the right to include whatever information it believes is necessary in a Federal Data Bank.	☐	☐	☐	☐	☐
B. Law enforcement agencies should be allowed access to all information that will aid in carrying out justice.	☐	☐	☐	☐	☐
C. A Federal Data Bank is threatening to individual privacy.	☐	☐	☐	☐	☐
D. Concern about the possibility of information stored in a Federal Data Bank being inappropriately released will lead to conformity in our society.	☐	☐	☐	☐	☐
E. An individual should be allowed to review and ·disagree with any information stored on him in a Federal Data Bank.	☐	☐	☐	☐	☐
F. A Federal Data Bank means that there will be more Federal control over the individual.	☐	☐	☐	☐	☐
G. A Federal Data Bank will enable the employer to make more accurate decisions on hiring and promoting workers.	☐	☐	☐	☐	☐
H. Centralization of information in a Federal Data Bank will tend to aid undesirable elements of society such as the underworld.	☐	☐	☐	☐	☐
I. A Federal Data Bank should include records on every individual residing in the United States.	☐	☐	☐	☐	☐

	Agree Strongly	*Agree*	*Neutral*	*Disagree*	*Disagree Strongly*
J. Release of data should be limited to the purpose for which the data was intended, except in emergency situations such as war or depression.	☐	☐	☐	☐	☐
K. People will tend to hide their activities if they know personal data will be fed into a centralized data bank.	☐	☐	☐	☐	☐
L. People should be allowed to conceal things from a Federal Data Bank.	☐	☐	☐	☐	☐
M. Release of information from a Federal Data Bank must have permission of the individual concerned.	☐	☐	☐	☐	☐
N. Centralization of information in a data bank provides greater opportunity for corruption of those Federal employees involved.	☐	☐	☐	☐	☐
O. Information from a Federal Data Bank about individuals should be made available to private industry.	☐	☐	☐	☐	☐
P. The Federal Government through the use of its Data Bank will be able to determine where discrimination in employment exists.	☐	☐	☐	☐	☐
Q. A Federal Data Bank means that there will be more Federal control over private industry and business.	☐	☐	☐	☐	☐
R. A Federal Data Bank can be a threat to your constitutional rights.	☐	☐	☐	☐	☐

Should you wish to make additional comments, please use the back of this page.

Name and address (if you wish)_____

Sex_____ Age_____

City or Community_____ Occupation_____

Last year of school completed_____.

                      a. Government

Type of employer (Circle)   b. Private Industry

                      c. Other_____

Had you ever heard of the Federal Data Bank before?_____

Articles in Addition to, and in Amendment of, The Constitution of the United States of America

Ten Original Amendments—The Bill of Rights

ARTICLE I.

Congress shall make no law respecting an establishment of religion, or prohibiting the free exercise thereof; or abridging the freedom of speech, or of the press; or of the right of the people peaceably to assemble, and to petition the Government for a redress of grievances.

ARTICLE II.

A well-regulated militia, being necessary to the security of a free State, the right of the people to keep and bear arms, shall not be infringed.

ARTICLE III.

No soldier shall, in time of peace be quartered in any house, without the consent of the owner, nor in time of war, but in a manner to be prescribed by law.

ARTICLE IV.

The right of the people to be secure in their persons, houses, papers, and effects, against unreasonable searches and seizures, shall not be violated, and no warrants shall issue, but upon probable cause, supported by oath or affirmation, and particularly describing the place to be searched, and the persons or things to be seized.

ARTICLE V.

No person shall be held to answer for a capital, or otherwise infamous crime, unless on a presentment or indictment of a Grand Jury, except in cases arising in the land or naval forces, or in the militia, when in active service in time of war or public danger; nor shall any person be subject for the same offense to be twice put in jeopardy of life or limb; nor shall be compelled in any criminal case to be a witness against himself, nor be deprived of life, liberty, or property, without due process of law; nor shall private property be taken for public use, without just compensation.

ARTICLE VI.

In all criminal prosecutions, the accused shall enjoy the right to a speedy and public trial, by an impartial jury of the State and district wherein the crime shall have been committed, which district shall have been previously ascertained by law, and to be informed of the nature and cause of the accusation; to be confronted with the witnesses against him; to have compulsory process for obtaining witnesses in his favor, and to have the assistance of counsel for his defense.

ARTICLE VII.

In suits at common law, where the value in controversy shall exceed twenty dollars, the right of trial by jury shall be preserved, and no fact tried by a jury, shall be otherwise reexamined in any court of the United States, than according to the rules of the common law.

ARTICLE VIII.

Excessive bail shall not be required, nor excessive fines imposed, nor cruel and unusual punishments inflicted.

ARTICLE IX.

The enumeration in the Constitution, of certain rights, shall not be construed to deny or disparage others retained by the people.

ARTICLE X.

The powers not delegated to the United States by the Constitution, nor prohibited by it to the States, are reserved to the States respectively, or to the people.

Automated Government—

How Computers Are Being Used in Washington to Streamline Personnel Administration to the Individual's Benefit—by John W. Macy, Jr.*

In any examination, whether in high school or college or in a civil service written test, it has never been considered cricket

---

* John W. Macy, Jr., is Chairman of the U.S. Civil Service Commission. This article appeared in *The Saturday Review*, July 23, 1966.

to show your paper to anyone else. In these days of automated examinations this same rule may be carried to the ultimate extreme: the only eyes that ever fall upon an applicant's civil service test may be his own. Even though the test may be sent across the continent, graded, and compared with the papers of other competitors, and even though the applicant may be hired and enter upon a lifetime career largely on the basis of this test, nobody but him need see it after he completes it.

This is one aspect of automation that bids to revolutionize personnel management in the federal government. Some may regard this feature as depersonalizing. But the truth is that mass examination scoring never was a highly personal activity. The automation of much personnel work of a clerical type may well serve to increase the personal attention managers can give to problems requiring human attention.

Automating examining techniques used by the U.S. Civil Service Commission may be both more advanced and more limited than the general public realizes. During fiscal 1966 the commission's computer automatically scheduled more than 700,000 applicants into 1,000 examination points throughout the nation, computed the scores of those who took these nationwide examinations, and notified applicants of the results. On the other hand, these high-volume figures deal only with nationwide written examinations. In many instances, persons who apply for positions are not tested, but rather are evaluated by a team of experts in a specific occupation, and are graded solely on their previous training and experience.

For one of the 700,000 persons who applies for an automated examination, the initial action on his part is simple and easy. He files only a small card form. In due course he receives an admission card, telling him to report at a specified date and hour at an examination point convenient to him. His examination has been scheduled by machine, and the time and location have been printed automatically. In the examination room, the competitor marks his answers to the questions by shading the appropriate block on a set of test-answer sheets. When the sheets are returned to the commission, computers then take over the next steps. Their output even includes a letter to the competitor notifying him of the test results.

The notification letters roll out of the computer in one long sheet, are mechanically separated, and are finally stuffed into mailing envelopes virtually untouched by human hands. Not only is this process immensely faster, it is more accurate and requires substantially smaller expense than processing by hand. In addition, the computer is programmed to check the validity of test results, to prepare studies showing how different groups of applicants performed on various sections of the examination, and to assist in establishing appropriate passing scores.

Automatic data processing has been applied to personnel management in the federal government for only about six years, yet the roots of the cybernetic revolution in government extend back to the 1880s. In fact, there is reason to think that the entire development of automatic data processing was initiated by an invention of a young Census Bureau employee appalled by the paper work of the 1880 tabulation.

Herman Hollerith was a young engineer working on the 1880 census. Seeing a need for something better than hand-work on the mass of census statistics, he put together a tabulating machine that he called his "statistical piano." It was somewhat reminiscent of a player piano, in that it used a roll of punched tape to feed instructions into the machine. People who, then as now, condemned the civil service for a lack of imagination and innovation, must have been looking the other way. Even the inventor may not have realized what he was starting, but in the 1890 census Hollerith's device was credited with saving two years of work and $5,000,000. Later it became the foundation for a phenomenal business—the company now usually referred to by the initials IBM.

The government also pioneered in the development and use of electronic data processing. One of the first completely electronic computers ever built was called ENIAC, for Electronic Numerical Integrator and Calculator. It was produced by the War Department and the University of Pennsylvania, working together in 1946 to solve problems in ballistic research. In 1951 the first commercial computer, UNIVAC I (Universal Automatic Computer), was installed in the Census Bureau, some three years before a private company put a UNIVAC into operation. The government received good value from its investment in UNIVAC I, running up more than 73,000 hours of operational use on the machine before retiring it to the Smithsonian Institution in October, 1963.

When first developed, the digital computer was used merely as a large and very fast calculating machine, or for complex accounting and statistical purposes. In government, priority was given to its employment in the primary mission of the agency by which it was used. By the early 1960s, however, the Department of Agriculture was using computer facilities for centralized personnel management data processing purposes. Its MODE (Management Objectives with Dollars through Employees) system is a large-scale centralized personnel record-keeping and reporting operation, utilizing a computer in New Orleans. In addition to records and reports, the system computes the pay checks for Agriculture's 100,000 employees throughout the nation.

The Veterans Administration, with 156,000 employees, was the second large agency to install a centralized, automated personnel system. This system, called PAID (Personnel and Accounting Integrated Data System), operates at Hines, Illinois. PAID encompasses general personnel management statistics and reports, career development and training records, a file on employees' length of service, payroll information to permit computation of checks by the machine, and information on the authorized number of positions as compared with the number of employees on the rolls. The system also contains a "suspense" file of personnel matters to be brought up on certain dates.

Twenty-two agencies of the government now have automated personnel systems covering 1,500,000 federal employees. Systems covering an additional 500,000 are being developed.

The Civil Service Commission first entered this field in administering the government-wide retirement system. Through an automated procedure, 750,000 retirement accounts are maintained with an annual increase of 45,000 new annuitants.

Three years ago a 5 per cent increase in all current annuities was authorized by Congress. This necessitated recomputation of the annuity for every person on the retirement rolls. The last time such a task was required it took months. The added workload was augmented by a stream of letters from Congressmen, justifiably wanting to know why their constituents were not receiving their higher retirement checks. But in 1963, thanks to the wondrous capability of the computer, 630,000 annuities were recomputed in just ten days and checks started flowing out before complaints and inquiries began pouring in.

The system is now being used to compute deductions for Medicare payments for those annuitants who are not receiving Social Security benefits. A recently completed management study of retirement and insurance operations indicated that over the next decade more than $3,000,000 can be saved through further automation.

Increased automation is to be expected. But it is time to ask searching questions about these systems and what they should be doing for us. Automated personnel systems put into use during the past few years are basically record-keeping and reporting systems. But it is a serious mistake to think of personnel offices primarily in terms of records and reports.

Personnel management is principally concerned with finding the best qualified people to fill vacancies, insuring maximum utilization of manpower resources, improving working conditions and thereby improving work—and providing equal employment opportunities to all our citizens, not only at the point of entrance into the service, but through training, promotions, and full career development. Seen from this perspective, automation of personnel operations is just beginning.

As we advance, the question facing us is this: Which parts of the job can a computer do better—and which can men do better? We know that a large part of management is actually clerical decision-making, though we have often dignified it in the past with the word "judgment." It requires the identification of relevant facts and the selection of predetermined actions on the basis of those facts. This a computer can do beautifully.

In scheduling civil service examinations, for example, our computer makes "decisions" of this kind by the thousands. Why should the time of a man or woman be devoted to such work with less accuracy and little satisfaction? We have other work for men and for women, in which they can do a far better job using the huge data resources of the computers. This work involves decisions on personnel planning, the matching of men and jobs, the forecasting of manpower needs, and the important decisions of career-planning.

For proper decisions in these areas we must have integrated information systems. This will require the use of information across departmental boundaries. It is here that current efforts to standardize symbols and codes will pay dividends. Direct tape-to-tape feeding of data from one department to another may become common. These systems will mesh well with developing plans for an executive-level staffing program which will be designed to locate the best possible man for any given top-level assignment, no matter where in government he may be serving.

The computer's ability to search its perfect memory and pick out records of individuals with specific characteristics has been applied in the search for candidates for Presidential appointments. A computerized file containing the names and employment data of some 25,000 persons, all considered likely prospects for federal appointive positions, is searched electronically. This talent bank, with its automated retrieval system, broadens the field of consideration for the President in critical decisions of leadership selection.

Throughout the government, one of the great responsibilities is to provide true equality of opportunity in employment. To know where we have failed to provide it, where we have succeeded, and how best to plan, we need a multitude of data. Through head-counts we know only that a certain number of Negroes, for instance, were on the rolls in certain grades at a certain time in the past, and now we can count that there are fewer or more. But these data do not reveal whether the people in certain jobs came from lower jobs or from outside the government. They do not assist us in recommending training or evaluating it. They fail to give us the management information required to do a conscientious job in creating conditions that will make a reality of equal opportunity.

To obtain additional and more accurate information, a new effort has been initiated in this area. By means of a voluntary racial designation prepared by employees themselves after employment, reliable information now can be fed into computers where it can be confidentially stored and used.

Most federal managers need more knowledge of computers in order to best use their capacities. With this in mind the commission last year established an ADP Management Training Center in Washington. More than 2,300 federal employees have attended its sessions.

There seems no doubt that increasing use of computers in government, accomplishing many of the clerical tasks by machine, will affect the skill requirements and the "occupational mix" of government service in the future. The Civil Service Commission has made an extensive study of this question, and is giving it continuing attention. Employee displacement has not been extensive; with intelligent planning an agency can prevent hardship for the employees affected.

An outstanding example is furnished by the Internal Revenue Service, which has done an exemplary job of minimizing the impact on employees in its extensive ADP conversion program through advance planning, and intensive retraining and placement efforts. This is the kind of personnel job no computer can handle.

This seems to me to be the answer to those who fear that computers will deemphasize humanity. Far from it! By removing the clerical decisions and the mass of paperwork details the computer may well free the mind of man for more worthy use.

Already it has heightened the need for imaginative and innovative managers who can grasp ideas, think in broad, philosophical terms, and apply such terms in decisions relating to public welfare. It has forced a finer degree of quantitative precision in executive judgment. It has liberated the manager to give his mind to greater scope of creativity. Rather than degrading the worth of the human being, the computer has placed a premium on man at his best.

The Day the Computers Got Waldon Ashenfelter

by Bob Elliott and Ray Goulding

The chroniclers of the life and times of Mary Backstayge, Noble Wife, of Steve Bosco the sportscaster, of the Piels brothers, and other almost fictional characters here prove that they can be as telling in print as on the air or the TV screen. Ashenfelter thought the computers would help him trap Y. Claude Garfunkel, but he was tripped up by his own shoe size.

A presidential commission has recommended approval of plans for establishing a computerized data center where all personal information on individual Americans compiled by some twenty scattered agencies would be assembled in one place and made available to the federal government as a whole.

Backers of the proposal contend that it would lead to greater efficiency, and insist that the cradle-to-grave dossiers on the nation's citizens would be used only in a generalized way to help deal with broad issues. Opponents argue that the ready availability of so much confidential data at the push of a computer button could pose a dangerous threat to the privacy of the individual by enabling the federal bureaucracy to become a monstrous, snooping Big Brother.

Obviously, the plan elicits reactions that are emotional, and cooler heads are needed to envision the aura of quiet, uneventful routine certain to pervade the Central Data Bank once it becomes accepted as just another minor governmental agency.

Fade in:

Interior — Basement GHQ of the Central Data Bank — Night. (At stage right, 950 sophisticated third-generation computers may be seen stretching off into the distance. At stage left, the CDB graveyard-shift chargé d'affaires, Nimrod Gippard, is seated behind a desk. He is thirty-five-ish and attired in socks that don't match. At the open, Gippard is efficiently stuffing mimeographed extortion letters to Omaha's 3,277 suspected sex deviates into envelopes. He glances up as Waldon Ashenfelter, an indoorsy type of questionable ancestry, enters.)

GIPPARD: Yes, sir?

ASHENFELTER (flashing ID card): Ashenfelter. Bureau of Indian Affairs. Like to have you run a check on a key figure named Y. Claude Garfunkel.

GIPPARD (reaching for pad and pencil): Sure thing. What's his Social Security number?

ASHENFELTER: I dunno.

GIPPARD: Hmmm. How about his zip code? Or maybe a cross-reference to some banks where he may have been turned down for a loan. Just any clue at all to his identity.

ASHENFELTER: Well, as I say, his name is Y. Claude Garfunkel.

GIPPARD (after a weary sigh): It's not much to go on, but I'll see what I can do.

(Gippard rises and crosses to the master data-recall panel. Ashenfelter strolls to a nearby computer and casually begins checking the confidential reports on his four small children to learn how many are known extremists.)

ASHENFELTER: You're new here, aren't you?

GIPPARD: No. Just my first week on the night shift. Everybody got moved around after we lost McElhenny.

ASHENFELTER: Wasn't he that heavy-set fellow with beady eyes who drove the Hudson?

GIPPARD: Yeah. Terrible thing. Pulled his own dossier one night when things were quiet and found out he was a swish. Kind of made him go all to pieces.

ASHENFELTER: That's a shame. And now I suppose he's gone into analysis and gotten himself cross-filed as a loony.

GIPPARD: No. He blew his brains out right away. But having a suicide on your record can make things tough, too.

ASHENFELTER: Yeah. Shows a strong trend toward instability. *(The computer informs Ashenfelter that his oldest boy was detained by police in 1963 for roller-skating on municipal property, and that the five-year-old probably founded the Farmer-Labor Party in Minnesota.)*

ASHENFELTER (cont.) (mutters in despair): Where did I fail them as a father?

GIPPARD: Didn't you tell me you're with Indian Affairs?

ASHENFELTER: Yeah. Why?

GIPPARD: I think I'm onto something hot. Is that like India Indians or whoop-it-up Indians?

ASHENFELTER: I guess you'd say whoop-it-up.

GIPPARD: Well, either way, no Indian named Garfunkel has ever complied with the Alien Registration Law.

ASHENFELTER: I never said he was an Indian. He's Jewish, and I think he's playing around with my wife.

GIPPARD: Gee, that's too bad.

ASHENFELTER (dramatically): Oh, I blame myself really. I guess I'd started taking LaVerne for granted and—

GIPPARD: No. I mean it's too bad he's only Jewish. The computers aren't programmed to feed back home-wreckers by religious affiliation.

ASHENFELTER: Oh.

GIPPARD: Can you think of anything kinky that's traditional with Jews? You know. Like draft dodging . . . smoking pot . . . something a computer could really hang its hat on.

ASHENFELTER: No. They just seem to feed each other a lot of chicken soup. And they do something around Christmastime with candles. But I'm not sure any of it's illegal.

GIPPARD: We'll soon see. If the curve on known poultry processors correlates geographically with a year-end upswing in tallow rendering— Well, you can appreciate what that kind of data would mean to the bird dogs at the ICC and the

FDA. They'd be able to pinpoint exactly where it was all happening and when.

ASHENFELTER: Uh-huh— Where and when what?

GIPPARD: That's exactly what I intend to find out.

(Gippard turns back to the panel and resumes work with a sense of destiny. Ashenfelter, whistling softly to himself, absently begins plunking the basic melody of "Mexicali Rose" on the keyboard of a nearby computer. The machine responds by furnishing him with Howard Hughes's 1965 income tax return and the unlisted phone numbers of eight members of a New Orleans wife-swapping club who may have known Lee Harvey Oswald. As Ashenfelter pockets the information, Major General Courtney ["Old Napalm and Guts"] Nimshaw enters. He has a riding crop but no mustache.)

NIMSHAW: Yoohoo! Anybody home?

GIPPARD: Back here at the main console.

(Nimshaw moves to join Gippard, then sees Ashenfelter for the first time and freezes. The two stand eyeing each other suspiciously as Gippard re-enters the scene.)

GIPPARD: Oh, forgive me. General Nimshaw, I'd like for you to meet Ashenfelter from Indian Affairs.

(Nimshaw and Ashenfelter ad-lib warm greetings as they shake hands. Then each rushes off to pull the dossier of the other. Ashenfelter learns that Nimshaw was a notorious bed wetter during his days at West Point and that his heavy drinking later caused an entire airborne division to be parachuted into Ireland on D-Day. Nimshaw learns that Ashenfelter owns 200 shares of stock in a Canadian steel mill that trades with Communist China and that he has been considered a bad credit risk since 1949, when he refused to pay a Cincinnati dance studio for $5500 worth of tango lessons. Apparently satisfied, both men return to join Gippard, who has been checking out a possible similarity in the patterns of poultry-buying by key Jewish housewives and reported sightings of Soviet fishing trawlers off the Alaskan coast.)

ASHENFELTER: Working late tonight, eh, General?

NIMSHAW (nervously): Well, I just stumbled across a little military hardware transport thing. We seem to have mislaid an eighty-six-car trainload of munitions between here and the West Coast. Can't very well write it off as normal pilferage. So I thought maybe Gippard could run a check for me on the engineer and brakeman. You know. Where they hang out in their spare time. Whether they might take a freight train with them. What do you think, Gipp?

GIPPARD: Sure. Just have a few more things to run through for Ashenfelter first. He's seeking a final solution to the Jewish problem.

ASHENFELTER (blanching): Well, not exactly the whole—

NIMSHAW: Oh, has all that come up again?

(Two janitors carrying lunch pails enter and cross directly to the computer programmed for medical case histories of nymphomaniacs. They pull several dossiers at random and then cross directly to a far corner, unwrapping bacon, lettuce, and tomato sandwiches as they go. They spread a picnic cloth on the floor and begin reading the dossiers as they eat. They emit occasional guffaws, but the others pay no attention to them.)

GIPPARD (as he compares graph curves): No doubt about it. Whatever those Russian trawlers are up to, it's good for the delicatessen business. This could be the break we've been hoping for.

NIMSHAW: Hating Jews has been a big thing with you for quite a while, Ashenfelter?

ASHENFELTER (coldly): About as long as you've been losing government property by the trainload, I imagine.

(Nimshaw and Ashenfelter eye each other uneasily for a moment. Then they quickly exchange hush money in the form of drafts drawn against secret Swiss bank accounts as Gippard's assistant, Llewelyn Fordyce, enters. Fordyce is a typical brilliant young career civil servant who has been lost for several hours trying to find his way back from the men's room. He appears haggard, but is in satisfactory condition otherwise.)

FORDYCE: Are you gentlemen being taken care of?

(Ashenfelter and Nimshaw nod affirmatively. Fordyce hurriedly roots through the desk drawers, pausing only to take a quick, compulsive inventory of paper clips and map pins as he does so.)

FORDYCE (cont.) (shouts): Hey, Gipp! I can't find the registry cards for these two idiots out here.

GIPPARD (faintly, from a distance): I've been too busy to sign 'em in yet. Take care of it, will you?

(Fordyce gives a curt, efficient nod, inefficiently failing to

realize that Gippard is too far away to see him nodding. Fordyce then brings forth two large pink cards and hands them to Nimshaw and Ashenfelter.)
FORDYCE: If you'd just fill these out please. We're trying to accumulate data on everybody who uses the data bank so we can eventually tie it all in with something or other.
(Nimshaw studies the section of his card dealing with maximum fines and imprisonment for giving false information, while Ashenfelter skips over the hard part and goes directly to the multiple-choice questions.)
FORDYCE (cont.): And try to be as specific as you can about religious beliefs and your affiliation with subversive groups. We're beginning to think there's more to this business of Quakers denying they belong to the Minutemen than meets the eye.
(Nimshaw and Ashenfelter squirm uneasily as they sense the implication. Ashenfelter hurriedly changes his answer regarding prayer in public schools from "undecided" to "not necessarily" as Nimshaw perjures himself by listing the principal activity at the Forest Hills Tennis Club as tennis. Meantime, Gippard has rejoined the group, carrying four rolls of computer tape carefully stacked in no particular sequence.)
GIPPARD: I know I'm onto something here, Fordyce, but I'm not sure what to make of it. Surveillance reports on kosher poultry dealers indicate that most of them don't even show up for work on Saturday. And that timing correlates with an unexplained increase in activity at golf courses near key military installations. But the big thing is that drunken drivers tend to get nabbed most often on Saturday night, and that's exactly when organized groups are endangering national security by deliberately staying up late with their lights turned on to overload public power plants.
FORDYCE (whistles softly in amazement): We're really going to catch a covey of them in this net. How'd you happen to stumble across it all?
GIPPARD: Well, it seemed pretty innocent at first. This clown from Indian Affairs just asked me to dig up what I could so he'd have some excuse for exterminating the Jews.
(Ashenfelter emits a burbling throat noise as an apparent prelude to something more coherent, but he is quickly shushed.)

GIPPARD (cont.): But you know how one correlation always leads to another. Now we've got a grizzly by the tail, Fordyce, and I can see "organized conspiracy" written all over it.

FORDYCE: Beyond question. And somewhere among those 192 million dossiers is the ID number of the Mister Big we're after. Do the machines compute a cause-and-effect relationship that might help narrow things down?

GIPPARD: Well, frankly, the computers have gotten into a pretty nasty argument among themselves over that. Most of them see how golf could lead to drunken driving. But the one that's programmed to chart moral decay and leisure time fun is pretty sure that drunken driving causes golf.

(Nimshaw glances up from the job of filling out his registry card.)

NIMSHAW: That's the most ridiculous thing I ever heard in my life.

FORDYCE (with forced restraint): General, would you please stick to whatever people like you are supposed to know about and leave computer-finding interpretation to analysts who are trained for the job?

(Nimshaw starts to reply, but then recalls the fate of a fellow officer who was broken to corporal for insubordination. He meekly resumes pondering question No. 153, unable to decide whether admitting or denying the purchase of Girl Scout cookies will weigh most heavily against him in years to come.)

FORDYCE (cont.): Any other cause-and-effect computations that we ought to consider in depth, Gipp?

GIPPARD: Not really. Of course, Number 327's been out of step with the others ever since it had that circuitry trouble. It just keeps saying, "Malcolm W. Biggs causes kosher poultry." Types out the same damned thing over and over: "Malcolm W. Biggs causes kosher poultry."

FORDYCE: Who's Malcolm W. Biggs?

GIPPARD: I think he was a juror at one of the Jimmy Hoffa trials. Number 327 was running a check on him when the circuits blew, and it's had kind of an obsession about him ever since.

FORDYCE: Mmmm. Well, personally, I've never paid much attention to the opinions of paranoids. They can get your thinking as screwed up as theirs is.

(Fordyce notices Ashenfelter making an erasure on his card

to change the data regarding his shoe size from 9½ C to something less likely to pinch across the instep.)

FORDYCE (cont.) (shrieks at Ashenfelter): What do you think you're doing there? You're trying to hide something from me. I've met your kind before.

(Ashenfelter wearily goes back to a 9½ C, even though they make his feet hurt, and Fordyce reacts with a look of smug satisfaction.)

GIPPARD: Maybe if I fed this junk back into the machine, it could name some people who fit the pattern.

FORDYCE: Why don't you just reprocess the computations in an effort to gain individualized data that correlates?

(Gippard stares thoughtfully at Fordyce for a long moment and then exits to nail the ringleaders through incriminating association with the key words "drunk," "poultry," "golf," and "kilowatt.")

NIMSHAW: I think maybe I'd better come back sometime when you're not so busy.

(He slips his registry card into his pocket and starts toward the door, but Fordyce grabs him firmly by the wrist.)

FORDYCE: Just a minute. You can't take that card out of here with you. It may contain classified information you shouldn't even have access to.

NIMSHAW: But it's about me. I'm the one who just filled it out.

FORDYCE: Don't try to muddy up the issue. Nobody walks out of this department with government property. Let's have it.

(Nimshaw reluctantly surrenders the card. Fordyce glances at it and reacts with a look of horror.)

FORDYCE (cont.): You've filled this whole thing out in long-hand! The instructions clearly state, "Type or print legibly." You'll have to do it over again.

(Fordyce tears up the card and hands Nimshaw a new one. Nimshaw, suddenly aware that a display of bad conduct could cost him his good conduct medal, goes back to work, sobbing quietly to himself.)

GIPPARD (faintly, from a distance): Eureka! Hot damn!

FORDYCE (happily): He's hit paydirt. I know old Gippard, and he hasn't cut loose like that since he linked Ralph Nader with the trouble at Berkeley.

(Gippard enters on the dead run, unmindful of the computer tape streaming out behind him.)

GIPPARD: It all correlates beautifully (ticks off points on his fingers). A chicken plucker. Three arrests for common drunk. FBI's observed him playing golf with a known Cuban. Psychiatric report shows he sleeps with all the lights on.

FORDYCE: All wrapped up in one neat bundle. Who is he?

GIPPARD: A virtual unknown. Never been tagged as anything worse than possibly disloyal until I found him. He uses the name Y. Claude Garfunkel.

ASHENFELTER: Y. Claude Garfunkel!

FORDYCE (menacingly): Touch a raw nerve, Ashenfelter?

(The two janitors, who are really undercover sophomores majoring in forestry at Kansas State on CIA scholarships, rise and slowly converge on Ashenfelter.)

GIPPARD: Want to tell us about it, Ashenfelter? We have our own methods of computing the truth out of you anyway, you know.

FORDYCE: No point in stalling. What's the connection? The two of you conspired to give false opinions to the Harris Poll, didn't you?

ASHENFELTER (pitifully): No! Nothing like that. I swear.

GIPPARD: Then what, man? What? Have you tried to sabotage the Data Bank by forging each other's Social Security numbers?

ASHENFELTER (a barely audible whisper): No. Please don't build a treason case against me. I'll tell. A neighbor saw him with my wife at a luau in Baltimore.

(The CIA men posing as college students posing as janitors react intuitively to jab Ashenfelter with a sodium-pentothol injection. Gippard rushes to a computer, where he begins cross-checking Garfunkel and Ashenfelter in the Urban Affairs file on "Polynesian power" advocates in Baltimore's Hawaiian ghetto and Interstate Commerce Commission reports on suspected participants in interstate hanky-panky. Fordyce grabs the red "hot line" telephone on his desk and reacts with annoyance as he gets a busy signal. General Nimshaw, sensing himself caught up in a tide of events which he can neither turn back nor understand, hastily erases the computer tape containing his own dossier and then slashes his wrists under an assumed name.)

Fade Out.

NOTES AND BIBLIOGRAPHY

Chapter I. The All-Seeing Eye

1. Frank K. Kelly, *Your Freedoms: The Bill of Rights*, New York, Bantam Books, 1966, pp. 102–103.
2. *Ibid.*, p. 108.
3. The *New York Times*, Dec. 7, 1967, p. 35.
4. John W. Macy, Jr., "Automated Government—How Computers Are Being Used in Washington to Streamline Personnel Administration to the Individual's Benefit," *The Saturday Review*, July 23, 1966, pp. 23–25, 70.
5. *The Computer and Invasion of Privacy*, Hearings before a Subcommittee of the Committee on Government Operations, House of Representatives, July 26–28, 1966, Washington, D.C., U.S. Government Printing Office, 1966, p. 2.
6. *Computer Privacy*, Hearings before the Subcommittee on Administrative Practice and Procedure of the Committee on the Judiciary, United States Senate, March 14–15, 1967, Washington, D.C., U.S. Government Printing Office, 1967, p. 2.
7. *Ibid.*
8. Speech given by Admiral Hyman Rickover before the Royal National Foundation of Athens, Greece, June, 1966. Reprinted in *The Computer and Invasion of Privacy, op. cit.*, p. 309.

9. *The Computer and Invasion of Privacy, op. cit.*, p. 3.
10. Oscar Ruebhausen and Orville Brim, Jr., "Privacy and Behavioral Research," *Columbia Law Review*, Vol. 65, Nov. 1965, p. 1194.
11. *The Computer and Invasion of Privacy, op. cit.*, p. 7.
12. *Ibid.*, p. 13.
13. *Ibid.*, pp. 311–318.
14. *The Wall Street Journal*, August 5, 1966, p. 6.
15. The New York *Post*, December 5, 1967, p. 22.
16. Arthur R. Miller, "The National Data Center and Personal Privacy," *The Atlantic Monthly*, Nov. 1967, p. 55.
17. Herman Kahn and Anthony J. Wiener, *The Year 2000: A Framework for Speculation on the Next Thirty-three Years*, New York, Macmillan, 1967, pp. 389–390.
18. *In the Matter of Regulatory and Policy Problems Presented by the Interdependence of Computer and Communication Services and Facilities*, a notice of inquiry by the Federal Communications Commission, Docket No. 16979, Nov. 9, 1966, p. 9.
19. *The Computer and Invasion of Privacy, op. cit.*, pp. 311–318.
20. Lynn White, Jr., "On Intellectual Gloom," *American Scholar*, Vol. 35, No. 2, Spring, 1966, p. 223.
21. *The Computer and Invasion of Privacy, op. cit.*, p. 4.
22. *Ibid.*, p. 5.
23. *Computer Privacy, op. cit.*, p. 264.
24. Paul Baran, *Communications, Computers and People*, Santa Monica, California, The RAND Corporation, Nov. 1965, p. 12.
25. *Computer Privacy, op. cit.*, p. 139.
26. Baran, *op. cit.*, p. 13.
27. *System Development Corporation Magazine*, Vol. 10, Number 7–8, July–August, 1967, p. 1.
28. W. H. Ferry, "Must We Rewrite the Constitution to Control Technology?" *The Saturday Review*, March 2, 1968, pp. 50–51.
29. *The Computer and Invasion of Privacy, op. cit.*, pp. 311–318.
30. Edward Shils, "Privacy and Power," reprinted in *Computer Privacy, op. cit.*, p. 246.

Chapter II. *The Proposed National Data Bank*

MAJOR REFERENCE: *The Computer and Invasion of Privacy*, Hearings before a Subcommittee of the Committee on Government Operations, House of Representatives, July 26–28, 1966, Washington, D.C., U.S. Government Printing Office, 1966.

1. John W. Macy, Jr., "Automated Government—How Computers Are Being Used in Washington to Streamline Personnel Administration to the Individual's Benefit," *The Saturday Review*, July 23, 1966, p. 25.
2. "Report of the Committee on the Preservation and Use of Economic Data to the Social Science Research Council, April 1965," in *The*

Computer and Invasion of Privacy. Hearings before a Subcommittee of the Committee on Government Operations, House of Representatives, July 26–28, 1966, Washington, D.C., U.S. Government Printing Office, 1966, p. 202.
3. "Statistical Evaluation Report No. 6—Review of Proposal for a National Data Center, Nov. 1, 1965," in The Computer and Invasion of Privacy, op. cit., pp. 254–278.
4. Ibid., p. 267.
5. Report of the Task Force on the Storage of and Access to Government Statistics, Washington, D.C., Oct. 1966, Executive Office of the President, Bureau of the Budget.
6. Computer Privacy, Hearings before the Subcommittee on Administrative Practice and Procedure of the Committee on the Judiciary, United States Senate, March 14–15, 1967, Washington, D.C., U.S. Government Printing Office, 1967, p. 10.
7. Arthur R. Miller, "The National Data Center and Personal Privacy," The Atlantic Monthly, Nov. 1967, p. 54.
8. Computer Privacy, op. cit., p. 137.
9. E. Glaser, D. Rosenblatt, and M. K. Wood, "The Design of a Federal Statistical Data Center," The American Statistician, Vol. 21, Feb. 1967, pp. 12–20.
10. John W. Macy, Jr., op. cit., p. 25.

Chapter III. The Keeper of Records: More Data Banks and Computer Installations

MAJOR REFERENCES: "Computers, How They're Remaking Companies," Business Week, Feb. 29, 1964; "The Computer in Society," Time, Vol. 85, No. 14, April 2, 1965, New York, pp. 85–91; "The Challenge of Automation," Newsweek, Jan. 25, 1965, pp. 73–80; Ben B. Seligman, Most Notorious Victory: Man in an Age of Automation, New York, Free Press, 1966; Don D. Bushnell and Dwight W. Allen, The Computer in American Education, New York, John Wiley and Sons, 1967; Gilbert Burck and eds. of Fortune, The Computer Age, New York, Harper and Row, 1965; Alice Mary Hilton, The Evolving Society, The Institute for Cybercultural Research, New York, ICR Press, 1966; Donald A. Laird and Eleanor C. Laird, How to Get Along with Automation, New York, McGraw-Hill, 1964.

1. The New York Times, June 4, 1968, pp. 61, 68.
2. Joe Alex Morris, "What the Credit Bureaus Know About You," Reader's Digest, Vol. 91, No. 547, Nov. 1967, pp. 85–90.
3. Hillel Black, Buy Now, Pay Later, New York, Wm. Morrow and Co., 1961.
4. "Prying for Pay: How Credit Bureaus Collect and Use Data on Millions of Persons," The Wall Street Journal, New York, Feb. 5, 1968, p. 1.

5. *System Development Corporation Magazine,* Vol. 10, No. 7–8, 1967, pp. 3–4.
6. "Prying for Pay: How Credit Bureaus Collect and Use Data on Millions of Persons," *op. cit.,* p. 16.
7. Joan and Leslie Rich, *Dating and Mating by Computer,* New York, Ace Books, 1966.
8. The *New York Times,* July 30, 1968, p. 41.
9. Ralph L. Bisco, "Social Science Data Archives: A Review of Developments," *The American Political Science Review,* Vol. LX, No. 1, March, 1966, pp. 93–109.
10. The *New York Times,* Jan. 14, 1967.
11. Donald N. Michael, Statement on Hearings on S.68 before the Senate Subcommittee on Intergovernmental Relations, Committee on Governmental Operations, Washington, D.C., U.S. Government Printing Office, 1967.
12. Louis Harris, in *American Psychologist,* Vol. 22, No. 11, Nov. 1967, pp. 1028–1029.
13. Herbert J. Gans, in *American Psychologist,* Vol. 22, No. 11, Nov. 1967, pp. 983–990.
14. The *New York Times,* Jan. 15, 1968, p. 27.
15. The *New York Times,* Dec. 29, 1967.
16. "Computers Put Speed into the Law," *Business Week,* Oct. 1, 1966, p. 196.
17. *System Development Corporation Magazine,* Vol. 10, No. 7–8, 1967, p. 12.
18. *Ibid.*
19. E. E. David, Jr., and R. M. Fano, "Some Thoughts About the Social Implications of Accessible Computing," *AFIPS,* Vol. 27, Part I, Proc. FJCC, Washington, D.C., Thompson Book Co., 1965, pp. 243–247.

Chapter V. *Babbage's Dream Come True: The Technical Feasibility*

MAJOR REFERENCES: Jeremy Bernstein, *The Analytical Engine,* New York, Random House, 1963; Charles H. Davidson and Eldo C. Koening, *Computers: Introduction to Computers and Applied Computing Concepts,* New York, John Wiley and Sons, 1967; Robert Arnold, Harold C. Hill and Aylmer V. Nichols, *Introduction to Data Processing,* New York, John Wiley and Sons, 1966; Alice Mary Hilton, *Logic, Computing Machines and Automation,* Cleveland and New York, World Publishing Co., Meridian Books, 1964; Pierre de Latil, *Thinking by Machine,* Boston, Houghton Mifflin Co., 1957; S. H. Hollingdale and G. C. Tootill, *Electronic Computers,* Middlesex, England, Penguin Books, 1965; *Automatic Data Processing Newsletter,* New York, The Diebold Group, Inc., Management Science Publishing, Inc., various issues 1964–1967.

1. David Sarnoff, "No Life Untouched," *The Saturday Review,* July 23, 1966, p. 21.

2. "Computers: How They're Remaking Companies," *Business Week*, Feb. 29, 1964.
3. Jean Mesnard, *Pascal: His Life and Works*, London, Harville Press, 1952.
4. John T. Merz, *Leibniz*, Edinburgh and London, Wm. Blackwood and Sons, 1934.
5. Charles Babbage, *Charles Babbage and His Calculating Engines: Selected Writings*, ed. by Philip and Emily Morrison, New York, Dover Publications, 1961.
6. Jeremy Bernstein, *The Analytical Engine*, New York, Random House, 1963, p. 52.
7. S. H. Hollingdale and G. C. Tootill, *Electronic Computers*, Middlesex, England, Penguin Books, 1965.
8. Edward Tomeski, "Personnel and Software: Third Generation EDP Dilemmas," *Administrative Management*, Vol. XXVIII, No. 3, March 1967, p. 17.
9. "The Computer Directory and Buyers' Guide—13th Annual Edition," *Computers and Automation*, Vol. 16, No. 6, June 1967.
10. *Automatic Data Processing Newsletter*, New York, The Diebold Group, Inc., Management Science Publishing, Inc., Vol. IX, No. 16, Jan. 4, 1965, p. 4.
11. Vernon H. Jensen, *Computer Hiring of Dock Workers in the Port of New York*, Reprint Series, No. 213, New York State School of Industrial and Labor Relations, Ithaca, New York, Cornell University, 1967, pp. 414–415.
12. S. H. Hollingdale and G. C. Tootill, *op. cit.*, p. 336.
13. The New York *Herald Tribune*, June 6, 1965.
14. *Time*, April 2, 1965, p. 84.
15. David Sarnoff, from "The Moral Crisis of Our Age," speech accepting an honorary doctoral degree of science, September 30, 1955.

Chapter VI. *Along the Road to Psychological Submission*

MAJOR REFERENCE: Jerry M. Rosenberg, *Automation, Manpower and Education*, New York, Random House, 1966.

1. Herman Kahn and Anthony J. Wiener, *The Year 2000: A Framework for Speculation on the Next Thirty-three Years*, New York, Macmillan, 1967, p. 89.
2. *The Wall Street Journal*, Sept. 15, 1965, p. 13.
3. "The Psychological Corporation MMPI Reporting Service," 1967 Catalogue, New York, Psychological Corporation.
4. Erich Fromm, *The Sane Society*, New York: Holt, Rinehart and Winston, 1955.
5. Jacques Ellul, *The Technological Society*, New York, Knopf, 1964.
6. Donald Michael, "Speculations on the Relation of the Computer to Individual Freedom and the Right to Privacy," *The George Washington Law Review*, Vol. 33, Oct. 1964, pp. 270–286.

7. Robert S. Lee, *System Development Corporation Magazine*, Vol. 10, No. 7 and 8, 1967, p. 7.
8. *Newsweek*, January 25, 1965, p. 77.
9. Kahn and Wiener, *op. cit.*, p. 351.
10. Floyd C. Mann, "Psychological and Organizational Impacts," in *Automation*, John T. Dunlop, ed. Englewood Cliffs, New Jersey, Prentice-Hall, Inc., 1962, p. 43.
11. Neil J. and William T. Smelser, eds., *Personality and Social System*, New York, John Wiley and Sons, 1963, p. 1.
12. Norbert Wiener, "Some Moral and Technical Consequences of Automation," *Science*, Vol. 131, 1960, p. 1356.
13. Einar Hardin and Gerald L. Hershey, "Accuracy of Employees Reports on Changes in Pay," *Journal of Applied Psychology*, Vol. 44, No. 4, 1960, pp. 269–275.
14. Lawrence K. Williams, "The Human Side of Systems Change," *Systems and Procedures Journal*, Vol. 15, No. 66, July–August, 1964, p. 42.
15. Ida R. Hoos, "When the Computer Takes Over the Office," *Harvard Business Review*, July–August, 1960, pp. 105–107.
16. Ben B. Seligman, *Most Notorious Victory: Man in an Age of Automation*, New York, Free Press, 1966, p. 218.
17. Walter Buckingham, *Automation: Its Impact on Business and People*, New York, Harper and Row, 1961.
18. Lawrence K. Williams, "How Automation Affects the White-Collar Clerical Employee," New York State School of Industrial and Labor Relations, Reprint, 1965.
19. Ida R. Hoos, "Impact of Automation on Office Workers," *International Labor Review*, Vol. 82, 1960, pp. 368–388.
20. *Automation*, London, Her Majesty's Stationery Office, 1956.
21. Floyd C. Mann, "Psychological and Organizational Impacts," in *Automation*, *op. cit.*, p. 63.
22. *Automation and the Middle Manager*, New York, American Foundation on Automation and Employment, Inc., 1966.
23. R. L. Martino, " 'Mind Stretching' for Management," *Automatic Data Processing Service Newsletter*, New York, The Diebold Group, Inc., Management Science Publishing, Inc., Vol. IX, No. 2, June 22, 1964, p. 1.
24. Simon Ramo, "A New Technique for Education," in Morris Philipson, ed., *Automation: Implications for the Future*, New York, Random House, 1962, pp. 428–442.
25. *Time*, April 2, 1965, p. 91.
26. *Ibid.*

Chapter VII. *The People React*

1. George Orwell, *1984*, New York, Harcourt, Brace and World, Inc., 1949, p. 267.
2. Frank K. Kelly, *Your Freedoms: The Bill of Rights*, New York, Bantam Books, 1966, p. 60.

3. *Time,* August 23, 1963, p. 53.
4. Herman Kahn and Anthony J. Wiener, *The Year 2000:* A Framework for Speculation on the Next Thirty-three Years, New York, Macmillan, 1967, p. 352.
5. *The Computer and Invasion of Privacy,* Hearings before a Subcommittee of the Committee on Government Operations, House of Representatives, July 26–28, 1966, Washington, D.C., U.S. Government Printing Office, 1966, p. 2.
6. Raymond Katzell, "Right of Privacy," *Virginia Law Weekly,* Vol. 17, No. 4, Oct. 15, 1964.
7. Richard S. Barrett, "Invasion of Privacy," *The Industrial Psychologist,* Division of Industrial Psychology of the American Psychological Association, Vol. 5, No. 2 and 3, Spring and Summer, 1968, pp. 39–44.
8. Thomas Rowan, in testimony before the House of Representatives, Subcommittee on Census and Statistics, Washington, D.C., U.S. Government Printing Office, 1966.
9. Robert Browning, "Paracelsus," in Edward Berdoe, *Browning's Message to His Time,* 4th ed., London, Swan Sonnenschein, 1897, p. 180.

Chapter VIII. Protecting Our Constitutional Rights

1. Pope Pius XII, in an address to the Congress of the International Association of Applied Psychology, Rome, April 10, 1958.
2. *Special Inquiry on Invasion of Privacy,* Hearings before a Subcommittee of the Committee on Government Operations, House of Representatives, June 2, 3, 4, 7, 23 and Sept. 23, 1965, Washington, D.C., U.S. Government Printing Office, 1966, p. 2.
3. *Ibid.,* p. 25.
4. Vance Packard, *The Naked Society,* New York, David McKay, 1964, p. 159.
5. *The Computer and Invasion of Privacy,* Hearings before a Subcommittee of the Committee on Government Operations, House of Representatives, July 26–28, 1966, Washington, D.C., U.S. Government Printing Office, 1966, pp. 28–29.
6. *Ibid.,* p. 183.
7. Andrew R. Burn, *Pericles and Athens,* Mystic, Connecticut, Verry Press, 1948, p. 72.
8. Frank K. Kelly, *Your Freedoms: The Bill of Rights,* New York, Bantam Books, 1966, pp. 15–19.
9. Joseph Story, *Commentaries on the Constitution of the United States,* Boston, 2nd ed., 1851, pp. 591, 597, 600.
10. Francis Lieber, *On Civil Liberty and Self Government,* London, 1853, pp. 44–47, 71–75, 224.
11. James Holbrook, *Ten Years Among the Mail Bags,* Philadelphia, 1855.
12. Lieber, *op. cit.,* pp. 103–105, 224–225.
13. Commonwealth v. Lovett, 4 Clark 5, Pennsylvania, 1831.

14. Alan Westin, *Privacy and Freedom*, New York, Atheneum, 1967, p. 339.
15. S. Warren and L. D. Brandeis, "The Right to Privacy," *Harvard Law Review*, 1890, p. 193.
16. 277 U.S. 438, 1928.
17. *Special Inquiry on Invasion of Privacy, op. cit.*, p. 4.
18. *Ibid.*
19. Westin, *Privacy and Freedom, op. cit.*, p. 342.
20. *Ibid.*, pp. 31–32.
21. Clinton Rossiter, "The Pattern of Liberty," in Konvitz and Rossiter, eds., *Aspects of Liberty*, Ithaca, New York, Cornell University Press, 1958, pp. 15–17.
22. Alan Westin, "Science, Privacy, and Freedom: Issues and Proposals for the 1970's," (Part I), *Columbia Law Review*, Vol. 66, June 1966, p. 1031.
23. Westin, *Privacy and Freedom, op. cit.*, p. 370.
24. Alan Westin, "Science, Privacy, and Freedom: Issues and Proposals for the 1970's," (Part II), *Columbia Law Review*, Nov. 1966, Vol. 66, No. 7, p. 1243.
25. Lopez v. United States, 373 U.S. 427 (1963).
26. *The Computer and Invasion of Privacy, op. cit.*, pp. 51–52.
27. *Ibid.*, p. 52.
28. *Ibid.*, p. 80.
29. *Time*, July 7, 1967, p. 59.
30. *In the Matter of Regulatory and Policy Problems Presented by the Interdependence of Computer and Communication Services and Facilities*, a notice of inquiry by the Federal Communications Commission, Docket No. 16979, Nov. 9, 1966, p. 7.
31. Lopez v. United States, 373 U.S. 427 (1963).
32. *The United Nations and Human Rights*, the eighteenth report of the Commission to Study the Organization of Peace, New York, August 1967, p. 44.
33. *Ibid.*, pp. 41–43.
34. *Ibid.*, p. 41.
35. *Ibid.*
36. *Computer Privacy*, Hearings before the Committee on the Judiciary, Subcommittee on Administrative Practice and Procedure, March 14–15, 1967, Washington, D.C., U.S. Government Printing Office, 1967, p. 132.
37. *Computer Privacy, op. cit.*, p. 139.
38. *The Computer and Invasion of Privacy, op. cit.*, p. 15.
39. William Douglas, in *The Great Rights*, Edward Cohn, ed., New York, Macmillan, 1963.

Chapter IX. The Transistorized Sherlock Holmes

1. Herman Kahn and Anthony J. Wiener, *The Year 2000: A Framework for Speculation on the Next Thirty-three Years*, New York, Macmillan, 1967, p. 98.

2. Vance Packard, *The Naked Society*, New York, David McKay, 1964.
3. Stanley Rothman, "Centralized Government Information Systems and Privacy," in *Computer Privacy*, Hearings before the Committee on the Judiciary, Subcommittee on Administrative Practice and Procedure, March 14–15, 1967, Washington, D.C., U.S. Government Printing Office, 1967, pp. 222–230.
4. Act of July 4, 1966, 80 Stat. 250.
5. "Clarifying and Protecting the Right of the Public to Information and for Other Purposes," Report No. 1210, Senate Committee on the Judiciary, 88th Congress, 2nd Session, 7, 1964.
6. Edward V. Long, *The Intruders: The Invasion of Privacy by Government and Industry*, New York, F. A. Praeger, 1967.
7. Packard, *op. cit.*
8. "California Statewide Information System Study," *Lockheed Missiles and Space Company Report*, p. G1–G4, July 30, 1965, Appendix G, Legal Considerations.
9. Alan Westin, *Privacy and Freedom*, New York, Atheneum, 1967, p. 386.
10. Paul Baran, *Communications, Computers and People*, Santa Monica, California, The RAND Corporation, Nov. 1965, P–3235.
11. *Computer Privacy*, Hearings before the Committee on the Judiciary, Subcommittee on Administrative Practice and Procedure, March 14–15, 1967, Washington, D.C., U.S. Government Printing Office, 1967, p. 162.
12. Bernard Peters, "Security Considerations in a Multi-Programmed Computer System," AFIPS, Vol. 30, Proc. SJCC, Washington, D.C., Thompson Book Co., 1967, pp. 283–286.
13. Willis H. Ware, *Security and Privacy in Computer Systems*, Santa Monica, California, The RAND Corporation, P–3544, April 1967.
14. H. E. Petersen and R. Turn, *System Implications of Information Privacy*, Santa Monica, California, The RAND Corporation, P–3504, April 1967.
15. Arthur Miller, "The National Data Center and Personal Privacy," *The Atlantic Monthly*, Nov. 1967, pp. 55–57.
16. *Ibid.*, p. 57.
17. Rothman, *op. cit.*, p. 229.
18. *The New York Times*, August 9, 1966.

Index

233) *Index*

ABOUT THE AUTHOR

JERRY M. ROSENBERG was formerly a Columbia and Cornell University assistant professor, teaching psychology and organizational behavior, and is now president of J. M. Rosenberg Associates, management and training consultants in New York City.

Dr. Rosenberg was graduated from the City College of New York, received an M.A. from Ohio State University in industrial psychology, and a Ph.D. from New York University. As a recipient of a Fulbright and French Government Grant he studied and was awarded a certificate from the Sorbonne's "Center of Higher Studies."

He is an associate member of Columbia University's Seminar on Technology and Social Change and is a member of the extension faculty, teaching applied psychology, at Cornell's Industrial and Labor Relations School in New York City.

Dr. Rosenberg is the author of several books, among them *Automation, Manpower and Education* and *The Computer Prophets*, as well as numerous articles for scholarly and popular journals.